D0552172

WEBER'S

Sizzle and Swizzle™

WEBER'S
Sizzle and Swizzle™

BARBECUED HORS D'OEUVRES
COOL COCKTAILS

SCOTT GIVOT

MQP

Published by MQ Publications Limited
12 The Ivories, 6–8 Northampton Street
London N1 2HY
Tel: 44 (0)20 7359 2244
Fax: 44 (0)20 7359 1616
email: mail@mqpublications.com
www.mqpublications.com

Copyright © 2005 Weber-Stephen Products
Illustration copyright © 2005 Marc Dando

Produced by MQ Publications Ltd under
exclusive licence from Weber-Stephen
Products Co.

MQ Publications:
Zaro Weil, CEO & Publisher

Weber-Stephen Products Co.:
Mike Kempster Sr., Executive Vice President
Jeff Stephen, Vice President Export Sales

Photography: Gus Filgate
Home Economy: Joy Skipper
Styling: Penny Markham
Recipe Credits: Scott Givot

ISBN: 1-84072-790-X

1 3 5 7 9 0 8 6 4 2

All rights reserved. No part of this publication
may be reproduced or transmitted in any form
or by any means, electronic and mechanical,
including photocopy, recording, or any
information storage and retrieval system now
known or to be invented without written
permission from the publishers.

Printed and bound in France by *Partenaires-Livres*®.

This book contains the opinions and ideas of the
author. It is intended to provide helpful and
informative material on the subjects addressed
in this book and is sold with the understanding
that the author and publisher are not engaged
in rendering any kind of personal professional
services in this book. The author and publisher
disclaim all responsibility for any liability, loss, or
risk, personal or otherwise, which is incurred
as a consequence, directly or indirectly, of the
use and application of any of the contents of
this book.

Introduction

In Summer I live on a small island. It is but one in a chain of archipelagos, having strayed from the mountainous mainland. The sea foams on its rocky shores and gulls squawk in delight with Neptune's bounty. Today the warm southwesterly winds prevail, while the sun languishes in luxurious white cumulus clouds. Sunset promises to be a glorious light show and the perfect backdrop to this evening's al fresco barbecue party.

I enjoy the company of my friends. Best of all is when we can make food together. It is 3 o'clock this July afternoon and although the guests will be arriving in two hours, the stage must be set. I have positioned the round cedar table and chairs at the back of the cottage, facing the anticipated slow dance of the setting sun on the waves. The barbecue is clean and a small work-table is positioned nearby to provide additional work-space. Nature takes care of most of the rest, thus, I need only to select the music, perhaps some gentle samba to set the tone? The travellers will be thirsty, so I have decided on the welcoming fruit drinks... tall, cool and refreshing in frosty glasses.

Today's party is easy on the host. All guests have been instructed to bring particular ingredients for a Latin American-style theme. This includes a variety of music, sparkling water, home-made coconut ice cream and a generous supply of passion fruit and fresh coriander. Everyone will be assigned a small task after they have quenched their thirst. Two will pick wild flowers, two will set the table and prepare additional beverages, one will preside over the barbecue and be responsible as DJ, while three of us will prepare the food.

I have selected a menu of five grilled items with savoury and spicy flavours. A pork selection has been marinating since last night and the chicken was rubbed in spices and refrigerated an hour ago. Together my helpers and I should be able to assemble and marinate the remaining ingredients within an hour's time. Once all of the ingredients are set up, we will gather round the barbecue and begin grilling. This food can be enjoyed in a relaxed fashion and at various intervals throughout the evening.

I believe this is the perfect way of entertaining. Let nature and its inhabitants create the atmosphere. As the host, I am responsible for nearly all the ingredients, the staging and a possible back-up plan, because accidents do happen and weather can go awry.

Enjoy the simplicity and informality of this book. Comprehensive instructions at the beginning of the book will bring you up to speed with your barbecue technique. Refer to it as needed and check it for tips, cooking time charts and safety instructions. Recipes for both food and drink are arranged by cultural families and complimentary ingredients and flavours. Given that we are a global society, feel free to mix and match the recipes. Above all, think simple, don't stress and JUST HAVE FUN WITH IT!

Barbecue Basics

CHARCOAL GRILLS

The secret of cooking on a charcoal kettle lies in the proper use of the lid and the vent system, along with two proven methods of positioning the charcoal briquettes. Air is drawn through the bottom vents to provide the oxygen necessary to keep the coals burning. The air heats and rises and is reflected off the lid, so it circulates around the food being cooked, eventually passing out through the top vent.

The art of charcoal barbecuing lies in mastering the fire – knowing how to set it up and how to control the temperature. Once you master that, it's easy and fun to cook entire menus and experiment with different combinations – and when you get the timing right, your guests will be able to enjoy all the food hot from the barbecue at the right time!

BUILDING THE FIRE

● **Use the right fuel:** solid hardwood charcoal briquettes are best. Look for either the square or round (also known as beads) types. Stay away from petroleum-based charcoal briquettes. They may last longer but they give off an unpleasant taste.

● **Use firelighters:** the waxy looking sticks or cubes – whenever possible, as they do not impart the chemical flavour often found when using lighter fluids. Firelighters also burn in all types of weather, ensuring a fast start to the fire. (If using lighter fluid, use it only on dry coals – never spray it on a lit fire!)

TIP

Always keep vents open. The wider the vent opening, the hotter the fire. At all times, remember to sweep ashes regularly so that the bottom vent stays clear.

LIGHTING YOUR GRILL

1. Remove the lid and open all of the air vents before building the fire. Spread the charcoal over the charcoal grate to determine how much you will need, then pile it into a mound in the centre of the grate.

2. Insert 4 firelighters (see **figure 1**), light them and let the coals catch alight and burn (see **figure 2**) until they are covered with a light grey ash. This usually takes about 20 to 25 minutes. You can also use a chimney starter (see the note on page 11).

3. Use tongs to arrange the coals on the grate according to the cooking method you are going to use.

● **For Direct cooking** (see **figure 3** and page 16), you should have an even layer of hot coals across the charcoal grate.

● **For Indirect cooking** (see **figure 4** and page 17), you should have enough coals to arrange them evenly on either side of the charcoal grate.

4. Finally, place the cooking grate over the coals, put the lid on and preheat the cooking grate for about 10 minutes. The grill is now ready to use.

figure 1

figure 2

figure 3

figure 4

HOW MUCH FUEL IS RIGHT?

Use the following charts for your initial settings, depending on the size of your barbecue. The best way to control the temperature of the barbecue is to adjust the number of coals. To get a hotter fire, add more coals to your initial settings. For a lower temperature, use fewer coals. This may require a little experimentation on your part, but eventually you will know what's right for your barbecue and the foods that you cook most often.

How many briquettes you need to use

BBQ kettle	Square traditional briquettes	Round charcoal beads
37cm diameter	15 each side	12–24 each side
47cm diameter	20 each side	28–56 each side
57cm diameter	25 each side	44–88 each side
95cm diameter	75 each side	4–8kg each side
Charcoal Go-Anywhere®	10 each side	12–24 each side

How many briquettes you need to add per hour for Indirect cooking

BBQ kettle	Number of coals per side / per hour
37cm diameter	6
47cm diameter	7
57cm diameter	8
95cm diameter	22
Charcoal Go-Anywhere®	6

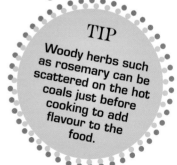

TIP

Woody herbs such as rosemary can be scattered on the hot coals just before cooking to add flavour to the food.

LIGHTING AGENTS

● **Firelighters:** Barbecue firelighters are waxy looking cubes or sticks, which are designed to light the barbecue without giving off any harmful fumes that could taint the food. Push four into the charcoal and light with a taper or a long stem match. They are easy to use, clean and safe. Only use firelighters designed for barbecues. Do not use firelighters designed for domestic fires as they contain paraffin, which will spoil the food.

● **Firelighter fluid:** If using this product you should handle with care. It should be sprayed on the dry coals, left for a few minutes to soak in, then ignited with a taper or long stem match. Never spray on hot or burning coals because the flames can travel up into the bottle causing serious burns.

CHIMNEY STARTER

A metal canister with a handle, a chimney starter holds a supply of charcoal. Crumpled newspaper or firelighters are put on the charcoal grate and lit, the chimney starter filled with coals is positioned over the firelighters. The walls of the chimney starter focus the flames and heat onto the charcoal, decreasing the amount of time it takes for the coals to light and ash over. Once the coals are ready, simply tip the coals onto the charcoal grate and arrange them for barbecuing.

EXTINGUISHING THE FIRE

1. Before you extinguish the coals, remove all food from the cooking grate and replace the lid. Allow the barbecue to continue heating the cooking grate until any smoking stops, 10 to 15 minutes, to burn off any cooking residues. Then give the grate a good brushing with a brass-bristle brush.

2. Close the lid and all the vents and let the barbecue cool down.

3. Do not handle hot ashes. Wait until they are cold, and remove them so they don't attract moisture and encourage rust. Some grills are equipped with blades that sweep the ashes into ash pans or catchers. Dispose of the ashes properly in a fireproof container. Always remove the ashes before storing a charcoal barbecue.

GAS GRILLS

Gas grills have one main advantage over charcoal and that's speed. Push the ignition switch and within about 10 minutes the barbecue is up to heat and ready to use. The workings of a gas barbecue are simple. First come burners to create heat, then some type of system above the burners to help disperse the heat, such as metal bars, lava rocks or ceramic briquettes. Above this is the cooking grate. Underneath the cooking box is a tray for collecting debris and fats.

Gas barbecues are run on Liquid Petroleum (LP) gas, which comes in two forms, butane or propane. The gas is under moderate pressure in the cylinder and is liquid. As the pressure is released the liquid vaporizes and becomes a gas.

LIGHTING YOUR GRILL

1. Check that there is enough fuel in your gas bottle (some barbecues have gauges to measure how much is left) and make sure that the burner control knobs are turned off.

2. Open the lid. Turn the gas valve on the bottle to 'on'.

3. Turn on the starter burner and light the grill according to the manufacturer's instructions using either the ignition switch or a match. When the gas flame has ignited, turn on the other burners.

4. Close the lid and preheat the grill until the thermometer reads 245 to 275°C. This takes about 10 minutes.

5. Using a brass-bristle brush, clean the grate to remove any debris left over from your last barbecue.

TIP
Always read the safety instructions carefully on transporting, storing and fitting gas bottles.

6. Adjust the burner controls according to the cooking method, Direct (*figure 5*) or Indirect (*figure 6*), you are going to use. The barbecue is now ready for cooking.

figure 5   figure 6

GETTING THE RIGHT TEMPERATURE

Most gas barbecues today have burner controls that are set to Low, Medium and High, but each model uses a different temperature, so be sure to learn what those are on your model. The recipes in this book are gauged to temperatures of about 150°C for Low; 180°C for Medium; and 245 to 275°C for High. Some gas barbecues have a built-in thermometer, but if yours does not, use an oven thermometer placed on the cooking grate.

TURNING THE FIRE OFF

1. Make sure all burners are switched to 'off'. Then, shut the gas down at the source.

2. When the barbecue has cooled down, preferably the next day, remove the catch pan from the bottom tray, or empty the drip tray so you don't get flare-ups or grease fires the next time you barbecue.

SMOKING

It's easy to add a more distinctive flavour to barbecued food by adding manufactured or natural flavourings to the smouldering coals, or the smoker box in the case of gas barbecues, before cooking. There are many types of flavoured woods and herbs available. They come in either chunks or chips, and should be soaked in cold water for at least 30 minutes prior to use.

- **On a charcoal barbecue:** Place the soaked chunks, chips or herbs directly on the hot coals. Add the food to the cooking grate and barbecue according to the recipe.

- **On a gas barbecue:** If your barbecue has a smoker box accessory, follow the manufacturer's instructions. If your barbecue does not have a smoker box accessory, simply place the chunks, chips or herbs in a small metal foil pan, cover with aluminium foil (poke holes in the foil to allow the smoke to escape) and place directly over the heat disbursement system or the cooking grate in one corner. Turn the grill on and, as it heats up, smoke will begin to form, and will flavour the food as it cooks. Never place the food directly over the pan of smoking materials.

weber Q AND weber baby Q

The Weber® Q™ is the first gas barbecue that can act as both a fully functioning barbecue for your garden and a portable gas barbecue.

Compact, just 46cm from front to back, and 80cm from handle to handle, the porcelain-enamelled cast-iron cooking grate lets you grill up to 10 king-size steaks or 15 burgers at the same time and a deep lid can cover a whole chicken.

The Weber® Q™ and Weber® Baby Q™ (see *figure 7* and the picture opposite) work in much the same way as other Weber gas barbecues with the exception that you cannot cook using the Indirect method on these grills. You can achieve a similar result by reducing the temperature to low and cooking larger cuts of meat on a roast holder. Where the cooking times and methods differ slightly than normal these are noted on the cooking time charts on pages 22–27 and in the grilling methods noted at the start of each recipe.

figure 7

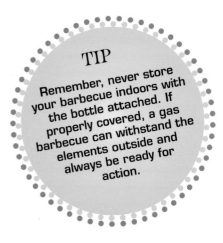

TIP

Remember, never store your barbecue indoors with the bottle attached. If properly covered, a gas barbecue can withstand the elements outside and always be ready for action.

LIGHTING WEBER® Q™ BARBECUES

1. Check that there is enough fuel in your gas bottle and that the burner control knob is turned off.

2. Open the lid and, on the Weber® Q™ gas grill, unfold the side tables.

3. Set the burner control knob to START/HI. Press the red igniter button to light the grill.

4. Close the lid and preheat the grill for about 10 minutes. The temperature will probably have reached approximately 245 to 275°C by this point.

5. Adjust the burner control knob according to the cooking method you are going to use.

EXTINGUISHING THE FIRE

1. To clean your cooking grate turn the burner control knob to HI and leave for about 10 minutes. Then brush the cooking grate with a brass-bristle brush.

2. Make sure the burner is switched to 'off'. Then, shut the gas down at the source.

3. When the barbecue has cooled down, preferably the next day, remove the catch pan from the bottom tray, or empty the drip tray so you don't get flare-ups or grease fires the next time you barbecue.

15

DIRECT COOKING

The Direct method means that the food is cooked directly over the heat source. To ensure that foods cook evenly, turn them only once, halfway through the grilling time. Direct cooking is also the best technique for searing meats. In addition to creating a wonderful caramelized texture and flavour, searing also adds grill marks to the surface of the meat. To sear meats, place them over Direct heat for 2 to 5 minutes per side. Remember that smaller pieces of meat require less searing time, and be especially mindful of too much searing on very lean cuts of meat as they can dry out quickly. After searing, finish cooking using the method called for in the recipe.

ON CHARCOAL

1. Prepare and light the coals as instructed on pages 8 to 9. Remember, don't begin to barbecue until the coals are covered in a light grey ash. Spread the prepared coals in an even layer across the charcoal grate.

2. Set the cooking grate over the coals, put the lid on and preheat the cooking grate for about 10 minutes. Place the food on the cooking grate and cover with the lid. The food will cook directly over the heat source (see *figure 8*).

3. Do not lift the lid during cooking time, except to turn the food once halfway through and to test for readiness.

ON GAS

1. To set up the barbecue for Direct cooking, first preheat with all burners on High. Once the barbecue is up to heat, usually about 10 minutes, adjust all burners to the temperature called for in the recipe.

2. Place the food on the cooking grate and close the lid. Again, the food will be cooked over the heat source (see *figure 9*).

3. Do not lift the lid during cooking time, except to turn the food once halfway through and to test for readiness.

figure 8

figure 9

INDIRECT COOKING

Indirect cooking is similar to roasting, but the barbecue adds flavour and texture that you can't get from the oven. The heat rises and reflects off the lid and inside surfaces of the barbecue to cook the food slowly and evenly on all sides. As in a convection oven, there is no need to turn the food over because the heat circulates around the food.

ON CHARCOAL

1. Prepare and light the coals as instructed on pages 8 to 9. Remember, don't begin to barbecue until the coals are covered in a light grey ash. Arrange the hot coals evenly on either side of the charcoal grate. Charcoal/fuel baskets or rails are accessories that keep the coals in place.

2. Place a drip pan in the centre of the charcoal grate between the coals to catch drippings. The drip pan also helps prevent flare-ups when cooking fatty foods such as duck, goose or fatty roasts. For longer cooking times, add water to the drip pan to keep the fat and food particles from burning.

3. Set the cooking grate over the coals, put the lid on and preheat the cooking grate for about 10 minutes. Place the food on the cooking grate over the drip pan and between the heat zones above the coals (see *figure 10*).

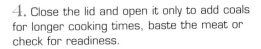

figure 10

4. Close the lid and open it only to add coals for longer cooking times, baste the meat or check for readiness.

ON GAS

1. Preheat the barbecue with all burners on High. Once the barbecue is up to heat, usually about 10 minutes, adjust the burners to the temperature called for in the recipe, turning off the burner(s) directly below the food.

2. Place the food on the cooking grate between the heat zones (see *figure 11*). For best results with roasts, poultry or large cuts of meat, use a roasting rack set inside a metal foil pan to catch the drippings.

3. Close the lid and open it only to baste the meat or check for readiness.

figure 11

17

BARBECUE HINTS AND TIPS

- **Stating the Obvious**

  Always make sure the barbecue is up to temperature before beginning to cook. For charcoal grilling, the charcoal should have a light grey ash on it for a good hot fire, which takes between 25 and 30 minutes. Use a chimney starter for best results. For gas grilling, first, open the lid (unfold the work surfaces on the Q™ gas grill), turn on the gas source, turn the burner control knobs to High (START/HI on the Q™ gas grill) and push a button to ignite the burner(s). Shut the lid, leave for about 10 minutes and you're ready to barbecue.

- **Down, Boy**

  Always cook with the lid of your barbecue down or on. This will reduce the chances of flare-ups and cook your food faster and more evenly. While cooking, resist the urge to open the lid to check on your dinner every couple of minutes. Every time you lift the lid, heat escapes causing your food to take longer to cook.

- **Don't Flip Out**

  Unless the recipe calls for it, flip your food just once.

- **Easy on the Squeeze**

  Resist the urge to use your spatula to press down on foods such as burgers or steaks. In doing this you'll only succeed in squeezing out all of the flavour, not making it cook faster.

- **Moisturize**

  A light coating of oil will help brown your food evenly and keep it from sticking to the cooking grate. Always brush or spray oil on your food, not the cooking grate.

- **Forego the Fork**

  Poking meat with a fork whilst cooking causes juices and flavour to escape and dries out your food. Just use the fork for lifting food from the grill and nothing more.

- **Cut It Out**

  Trim excess fat from steaks, chops, and roasts leaving no more than a scant 5mm thick layer.

- **Adjust to Your Environment**

  Grilling times listed in the recipes are approximate. Allow more time on cold or windy days or at higher altitudes.

- **Procrastinate**

  When using a marinade or glaze with a high sugar content or other ingredients that burn easily, brush on food only during the last 10 to 15 minutes of cooking.

- **Is Dinner Ready Yet?**

  A kitchen timer and an instant-read

thermometer are your best defenses against overcooked foods. Use the thermometer to check on readiness in roasts, or thick cuts of meat, but never leave it in the food while cooking.

- **Every Time You Grill**
  Do the burn off. On a gas grill, turn all of the burners on high, close the lid, leave for about 10 to 15 minutes, then brush the cooking grates thoroughly with a brass-bristle, long-handled grill brush (use a steel brush on cast-iron grates). For a charcoal grill, unless you have a very hot fire going when you are finished barbecuing, it's easier to clean your cooking grate right before you begin cooking – after the grate has pre-heated.

SAFE SIZZLE

- Always keep the barbecue at least 3m away from any combustible materials including the house, garage and fences.

- Do not use the grill indoors or under a covered patio, open garage door or carport.

- Keep children and pets away from a hot barbecue at all times.

- Do not add lighter fluid to a lit fire.

- Make sure the barbecue is sturdy; do not use if it wobbles, or is otherwise unstable. Always stand the barbecue on a level surface.

- Use heat-resistant barbecue mitts and long-handled tongs to turn the food.

- Do not spray oil on a hot cooking grate; oil the food instead.

- Do not use water to extinguish a flare-up. Close the lid (and all vents on a charcoal grill) to reduce the oxygen flow and eliminate flare-ups. If necessary, turn a gas grill off at the source. Keep a fire extinguisher handy in case of a mishap.

- Do not store propane tanks indoors or in the garage.

- Do not line the bottom of a barbecue or cover the cooking grate with foil. This obstructs airflow and also collects grease, which can result in flare-ups.

- When finished barbecuing, close the lid and all vents on a charcoal barbecue; close the lid and turn off all burners and the LP tank or source on a gas grill. Make sure that hot coals are fully extinguished before leaving the barbecue site.

FOOD SAFETY

● Defrost meat, fish and poultry only in the refrigerator, never at room temperature.

● Allow meats to come to room temperature before cooking, but do not do so in a room that is over 21°C. Do not place raw food in direct sunlight or near a heat source.

● When using a sauce during barbecuing, divide it in half and keep one part separate for serving with the finished dish. Use the other half for basting the meat; do not use this as a sauce for serving. If using a marinade that was used on raw meats, fish or poultry, boil it vigorously for at least 1 full minute before using it as a baste or sauce.

● Do not place cooked food on the same dish that the raw food was placed on prior to cooking.

● Wash all dishes, plates, cooking utensils, barbecuing tools and work surfaces that have come into contact with raw meats or fish with hot soapy water. Wash your hands thoroughly after handling raw meats or fish.

● Chill any leftover cooked food from the barbecue once it has cooled.

● Always barbecue minced meats to at least 71°C (77°C for poultry), the temperature for medium (well done) readiness.

ACCESSORIES

For best results, use the right tools when barbecuing. Here is a list of some of the essentials:

• Wide metal spatula – used for turning chicken pieces, vegetables and smaller pieces of food.

• Long-handled grill brush – preferably with brass bristles, to keep the grates clean without scratching the porcelain enamel. A steel-bristle brush is best for cleaning cast-iron grates.

• Basting brush – used for basting food with marinade or oil. Best with natural bristles (nylon bristles will melt if they touch the cooking grate) and a long handle.

• Long-handled tongs – used for turning sausages, shellfish, kebabs, etc.

• Long-handled fork – used for lifting cooked roasts and whole poultry from the barbecue.

• Barbecue mitts/oven gloves – these should be long-sleeved, flame-resistant gloves to protect your hands and forearms.

• Skewers – wooden or metal skewers are excellent for holding small pieces of meat, fish or vegetables and make it easy to turn food quickly on the barbecue, ensuring faster cooking. Remember to soak wooden

skewers, if using them, in cold water for at least 30 minutes before adding the food.

• Meat thermometer – used for best results every time, a thermometer takes the guess work out of judging if food is cooked.

• Timer – an excellent tool, so you don't have to watch the clock and can continue preparing other parts of the meal while the food is cooking.

• Foil drip pans – these keep the base of the barbecue clean and gather fats and juices that fall from the food during cooking.

• Roast holder – when cooking large cuts of meat and poultry on a gas barbecue, a roast holder in a foil pan will catch the drippings and reduce the chance of flare-ups.

TIP

Long-handled equipment not only makes the job safer but also quicker and more efficient.

BARBECUE GUIDES

The following thicknesses, weights and barbecue times are meant to be general guidelines rather than firm rules and you may notice that recipe times vary in comparison. When following a recipe, always follow the specific instructions. Cooking times are affected by wind, outside temperature and desired degree of cooking.

KEY TO METHOD OF COOKING

In the following fish, meat, poultry, vegetable and fruit cooking charts the approximate cooking time is followed by the barbecue method. These methods are also referred to throughout the book. Note: when cooking on Weber® Q™ or Baby Q™ always turn food once halfway through cooking, even if using a roast holder.		
DL	Direct Low Heat
DM	Direct Medium Heat
DH	Direct High Heat
IL	Indirect Low Heat
IM	Indirect Medium Heat
IH	Indirect High Heat

Fish & Seafood	Thickness/Weight	Grilling Time for Gas/Charcoal	Grilling Time for Weber® Q™ and Baby Q™
Fish fillet or steak	5mm to 1cm thick	3 to 5 minutes DH	3 to 5 minutes DH
	1 to 2.5cm thick	5 to 10 minutes DH	5 to 10 minutes DH
	2.5 to 3cm thick	10 to 12 minutes DH	10 to 12 minutes DH
Fish, whole	450g	15 to 20 minutes IM	15 to 20 minutes DM
	900 to 1.1kg	20 to 30 minutes IM	20 to 30 minutes DM
	1.4kg	30 to 45 minutes IM	
Fish kebab	2.5cm thick	8 to 10 minutes DM	8 to 10 minutes DM
Prawn		2 to 4 minutes DH	2 to 4 minutes DH
Scallop		3 to 6 minutes DH	3 to 6 minutes DH
Mussel (discard any that do not open)		5 to 6 minutes DH	5 to 6 minutes DH
Clam (discard any that do not open)		8 to 10 minutes DH	8 to 10 minutes DH
Oyster		3 to 5 minutes DH	3 to 5 minutes DH
Lobster tail		7 to 11 minutes DM	7 to 11 minutes DM

Note: General rule for grilling fish: 4 to 5 minutes per 1cm thickness; 8 to 10 minutes per 2.5cm thickness.

Beef	Thickness/Weight	Grilling Time for Gas/Charcoal	Grilling Time for Weber® Q™ and Baby Q™
Steak: sirloin, T-bone or rib	2.5cm thick	6 to 8 minutes DH	6 to 8 minutes DH
	3cm thick	8 to 10 minutes DH	8 to 10 minutes DH
	4cm thick	12 to 16 minutes total; sear 8 to 10 minutes cook 4 to 6 minutes IH	12 to 16 minutes total; sear 8 to 10 minutes DH, cook 4 to 6 minutes DL
	5cm thick	18 to 22 minutes total; sear 8 to 10 minutes DH, cook 10 to 12 minutes IH	
Skirt steak	5mm to 1cm thick	4 to 6 minutes DH	4 to 6 minutes DH
Flank steak	650 to 900g 2cm thick	8 to 10 minutes DH	8 to 10 minutes DH
Kebab	2.5 to 4cm cubes	7 to 8 minutes DH	7 to 8 minutes DH
Tenderloin, whole	1.5 to 1.75kg	35 to 50 minutes total; sear 15 minutes DM, cook 20 to 30 minutes IM	45 to 50 minutes (medium rare); sear 12 minutes DH (turn 4 times), cook 33 to 38 minutes DL
Minced beef burger	2cm thick	8 to 10 minutes DH	8 to 10 minutes DM
Rib roast (prime rib), boneless	2.25kg to 2.75kg	1¼ to 1¾ hours IM	1½ to 2 hours DL (on roasting rack) – on Q™ grill only
Strip loin roast, boneless	1.75kg to 2.25kg	45 to 60 minutes total; sear 2 to 4 minutes DH, cook 45 to 60 minutes IM	
Veal loin chop	2.5cm thick	6 to 8 minutes DH	6 to 8 minutes DH

Note: All cooking times are for medium-rare readiness, except ground beef and ground lamb (medium).

Safe Cooking Temperature for Beef
Cook beef roasts and steaks to 62°C for medium rare (71°C for medium) / cook minced beef to at least 71°C.

Pork	Thickness/Weight	Grilling Time for Gas/Charcoal	Grilling Time for Weber® Q™ and Baby Q™
Bratwurst, fresh		20 to 25 minutes DM	25 to 30 minutes DL
Bratwurst, pre-cooked		10 to 12 minutes DM	10 to 12 minutes DM
Pork chop, boneless or bone-in	1cm thick	5 to 7 minutes DH	5 to 8 minutes DH
	2cm thick	6 to 8 minutes DH	
	2.5cm thick	8 to 10 minutes DM	8 to 10 minutes DM
	3 to 4cm thick	10 to 12 minutes total; sear 6 minutes DH, cook 4 to 6 minutes IM	14 to 18 minutes total; sear 8 minutes DH, cook 6 to 10 minutes DL
Loin roast, boneless	1kg	40 to 45 minutes DM	
Loin roast, bone-in	1.25 to 2.25kg	1$^1/_4$ to 1$^3/_4$ hours IM	1$^1/_4$ to 1$^3/_4$ hours DL (on roasting rack) – on Q™ only
Pork shoulder, boneless	2.25 to to 2.75kg	3$^1/_2$ to 4 hours DL	
Pork, minced	2cm thick	8 to 10 minutes DM	8 to 10 minutes DM
Ribs, baby back	700 to 900g	1$^1/_2$ to 2 hours IL	See directly below
Ribs, spareribs	1.25 to 2.25kg	2$^1/_2$ to 3 hours IL	1$^1/_4$ to 1$^1/_2$ hours DL (on rib rack) – on Q™ only
Ribs, country-style, boneless	700 to 900g	12 to 15 minutes DM	
Ribs, country-style	1.25 to 1.75kg	1$^1/_2$ to 2 hours IM	
Tenderloin, whole	350 to 450g	15 to 20 minutes DM	25 to 30 minutes total; sear 10 minutes DH (turn 3 times), then cook 15 to 20 minutes DL

Safe Cooking Temperature for Pork

Cook all pork to 71°C.

Safe Cooking Temperature for Lamb

Cook lamb to 62°C for medium rare (71°C for medium) / cook minced lamb to 71°C.

Safe Cooking Temperature for Poultry

Cook whole poultry to 82°C / cook minced poultry to 74°C / cook chicken breasts to 77°C / cook duck and goose to 82°C.

Lamb	Thickness/Weight	Grilling Time for Gas/Charcoal	Grilling Time for Weber® Q™ and Baby Q™
Chop: loin, rib, shoulder, or sirloin	2cm to 3cm thick	8 to 12 minutes DM	8 to 12 minutes DM
Leg of lamb roast, boneless	2.25 to 3.25kg	$1^1/_4$ to $1^3/_4$ hours IM	2 to $2^1/_2$ hours DL (on roasting rack) – on Q™ only
Leg of lamb, butterflied	1.25 to 1.5kg	$1^1/_4$ to $1^1/_2$ hours total; sear 10 to 15 minutes DM, cook 1 to $1^1/_4$ hours IM	
Rib crown roast	1.25 to 1.75kg	1 to $1^1/_4$ hours IM	
Minced lamb burger	2cm thick	8 to 10 minutes DM	8 to 10 minutes DM
Rack of lamb	450 to 700g	20 to 30 minutes DM	20 to 30 minutes DM

Note: All cooking times are for medium-rare readiness, except ground beef and ground lamb (medium).

Poultry	Thickness/Weight	Grilling Time for Gas/Charcoal	Grilling Time for Weber® Q™ and Baby Q™
Chicken breast, boneless, skinless	175g	8 to 12 minutes DM	8 to 12 minutes DM
Chicken thigh, boneless, skinless	115g	8 to 10 minutes DH	8 to 10 minutes DH
Chicken pieces, bone-in breast/wing		30 to 40 minutes IM	30 to 40 minutes DL
Chicken pieces, bone-in leg/thigh		40 to 50 minutes IM	40 to 50 minutes DL
Chicken, whole	1.5 to 2.25kg	1 to $1^1/_2$ hours IM	1 to $1^1/_2$ hours DL (on roasting rack) – on Q™ grill only
Chicken kebab	2.5cm thick	6 to 8 minutes DM	6 to 8 minutes DM
Cornish game hen	700 to 900g	30 to 45 minutes IM	30 to 35 minutes DL
Turkey breast, boneless	1.25kg	1 to $1^1/_4$ hours IM	
Turkey, whole, unstuffed	4.5 to 5kg	$1^3/_4$ to $2^1/_2$ hours IM	
	5.5 to 6.5kg	$2^1/_4$ to 3 hours IM	
	6.75 to 7.75kg	$2^3/_4$ to $3^3/_4$ hours IM	
	8 to 10kg	$3^1/_2$ to 4 hours IM	
Duck breast, boneless	200 to 225g	12 to 15 minutes DL	12 to 15 minutes DL
Duck, whole	2.25 to 2.75kg	40 minutes IH	

Vegetables	Grilling Time for Gas/Charcoal	Grilling Time for Weber® Q™ and Baby Q™
Artichoke, whole	boil 12 to 15 minutes; cut in half and grill 4 to 6 minutes DM	boil 12 to 15 minutes; cut in half and grill 4 to 6 minutes DM
Asparagus	6 to 8 minutes DM	6 to 8 minutes DM
Aubergine, 1cm slices	8 to 10 minutes DM	8 to 10 minutes DM
Aubergine, halved	12 to 15 minutes DM	12 to 15 minutes DM
Beet	1 to $1^1/_2$ hours IM	1 to $1^1/_2$ hours DL
Corn, husked	10 to 15 minutes DM	10 to 12 minutes DM
Corn, in husk	25 to 30 minutes DM	25 to 30 minutes DM
Courgette, 1cm slices	6 to 8 minutes DM	6 to 8 minutes DM
Courgette, halved	6 to 10 minutes DM	6 to 10 minutes DM
Fennel, 5mm slices	10 to 12 minutes DM	10 to 12 minutes DM
Garlic, whole	45 to 60 minutes IM	45 to 60 minutes DL
Green bean, whole	8 to 10 minutes DM	8 to 10 minutes DM
Green onion, whole	3 to 4 minutes DM	3 to 4 minutes DM
Leek, halved	steam 4 to 5 minutes; grill 3 to 5 minutes DM	steam 4 to 5 minutes; grill 3 to 5 minutes DM
Mushroom: shiitake or button	8 to 10 minutes DM	8 to 10 minutes DM
Mushroom: portabello	10 to 15 minutes DM	10 to 15 minutes DM
Onion, halved	35 to 40 minutes IM	
Onion, 1cm slices	8 to 12 minutes DM	8 to 12 minutes DM
pepper, whole	10 to 15 minutes DM	10 to 12 minutes DM
pepper, 5mm slices	6 to 8 minutes DM	6 to 8 minutes DM
Potato, whole	45 to 60 minutes IM	45 to 60 minutes DL
Potato, 1cm slices	14 to 16 minutes DM	14 to 16 minutes DM
Potato: new, halved	15 to 20 minutes DM	15 to 20 minutes DM
Pumpkin (1.25kg), halved	$1^1/_2$ to 2 hours IM	$1^1/_2$ to 2 hours DL
Squash: acorn (450g), halved	1 to $1^1/_4$ hours IM	1 to $1^1/_4$ hours DL
Squash: butternut (900g), halved	50 to 55 minutes IM	50 to 55 minutes DL
Squash: patty pan	10 to 12 minutes DM	10 to 12 minutes DM
Squash: yellow, 1cm slices	6 to 8 minutes DM	6 to 8 minutes DM
Squash: yellow, halved	6 to 10 minutes DM	6 to 10 minutes DM
Sweet potato, whole	50 to 60 minutes IM	50 to 60 minutes DL
Sweet potato, 5mm slices	8 to 10 minutes DM	8 to 10 minutes DM

Vegetables	Grilling Time for Gas/Charcoal	Grilling Time for Weber® Q™ and Baby Q™
Tomato: garden, 1cm slices	2 to 4 minutes DM	2 to 4 minutes DM
Tomato: garden, halved	6 to 8 minutes DM	6 to 8 minutes DM
Tomato: plum, halved	6 to 8 minutes DM	6 to 8 minutes DM
Tomato: plum, whole	8 to 10 minutes DM	8 to 10 minutes DM

Fruit	Grilling Time for Gas/Charcoal	Grilling Time for Weber® Q™ and Baby ™
Apple, whole	35 to 40 minutes IM	
Apple, 1cm thick slices	4 to 6 minutes DM	4 to 6 minutes DM
Apricot, halved, pit removed	6 to 8 minutes DM	6 to 8 minutes DM
Banana, halved lengthways	6 to 8 minutes DM	6 to 8 minutes DM
Nectarine, halved lengthways, pit removed	8 to 10 minutes DM	8 to 10 minutes DM
Peach, halved lengthways, pit removed	8 to 10 minutes DM	8 to 10 minutes DM
Pear, halved lengthways	10 to 12 minutes DM	10 to 12 minutes DM
Pineapple, peeled and cored, 1cm slices or 2.5cm wedges	5 to 10 minutes DM	5 to 10 minutes DM
Strawberry	4 to 5 minutes DM	4 to 5 minutes DM

Note: Grilling times for fruit will depend on ripeness.

COCONUT MILK

A coconut-flavoured liquid made by pouring boiling water over shredded coconut, which is then cooled and strained. This creamy milk is most associated with Thai cooking.

Flavours

CHILLI SAUCE

These fiery sauces can be bought in a variety of flavours and degrees of heat. They really add a punch to marinades and are perfect for adding a bit of sizzle to your barbecue meal.

CORIANDER

The leaves have quite a strong flavour when fresh and can be used to sharpen up any recipe. The seeds are a wonderful blend of white pepper, cardamom and cloves.

PINEAPPLE

These are delicious prepared in any number of ways, but you can't beat it grilled on the barbecue with some tangy rum butter.

OLIVES

Olives are small bitter oval fruit, green when unripe and black when ripe. They are perfect as a simple pre-dinner hors d'oeuvres, but can also be a useful flavour to add to marinades and sauces.

PAPRIKA

Like all capsicums, the paprika varieties are native to South America, although it is now grown in Hungary and Spain. The main thing to remember when cooking with paprika, is that it only releases its colour and smoky flavour when heated – so although sprinkling it over a dish will make it look attractive it will not actually add any flavour unless it is used within the recipe, such as in rubs and marinades.

CHAPTER ONE

Latin & Caribbean

Mini Quesadillas

Gas Direct Medium Heat / **Weber® Q™** Direct Medium Heat / **Charcoal** Direct
Prep time 20 minutes / **Grilling time** 5 minutes / **Serves** 8

**8 flour tortillas 25cm
  across**
**225g mature Cheddar or
  Gouda cheese, grated**
**6 plum tomatoes, diced into
  small cubes, liquid drained**
¼ teaspoon coarse sea salt
**2 jalapeño chillies, deseeded
  and finely chopped**
**25g fresh coriander,
  coarsely chopped**
**2 tablespoons melted
  butter**
2 tablespoons olive oil

1. To prepare the quesadillas: lay a tortilla flat on a chopping board. Beginning with the cheese, sprinkle each ingredient, apart from the butter, in layers over half the tortilla. Fold the uncovered half over as if closing a book and press gently.

2. Melt the butter and olive oil in a small pan and brush over the top of the quesadillas. Grill, buttered side down, over Direct Medium heat for 5 minutes, turning once halfway through. Brush the other side with the remaining butter and olive oil after turning.

3. To serve, transfer the quesadillas to a chopping board and slice into wedges. Arrange on a platter and caution guests about molten-hot cheese.

Havana Beach

**2 parts golden or white
  Cuban rum**
3 parts pineapple juice
1 teaspoon sugar syrup
Ginger ale
Pineapple cube, to garnish

Shake the rum, pineapple juice and sugar syrup vigorously in a cocktail shaker with cracked ice. Strain into an old-fashioned glass, half-filled with ice cubes. Top up with ginger ale. Garnish with a few pineapple cubes.

Montego Bay Jerk Chicken Skewers

Gas Direct High Heat / **Weber® Q™** Direct High Heat / **Charcoal** Direct
Prep time 20 minutes + 2 hours marinating / **Grilling time** 4 minutes / **Serves** 8

**675g skinless chicken
  breast or thigh fillets
3 tablespoons melted
  butter, for basting
Several wooden skewers
  soaked in cold water for
  30 minutes**

For the marinade:
**1 to 3 Scotch bonnets or
  Habanero chillies,
  stemmed and deseeded,
  depending on desired heat
  (caution: these are HOT!)
1 small onion, coarsely
  chopped
3 garlic cloves, coarsely
  chopped
1 tablespoon fresh root
  ginger, coarsely chopped
15g fresh coriander
½ teaspoon ground
  cinnamon
½ teaspoon ground cloves**

1. To prepare the marinade: combine all the ingredients in a blender or food processor and process into a coarse paste. Leave to rest at room temperature while preparing the chicken.

2. Rinse the chicken thoroughly under cold running water; pat dry with kitchen paper. Cut into strips 5 x 10cm and place in a shallow dish. Pour the marinade over the chicken and toss until fully coated. Cover with clingfilm and refrigerate for 2 hours.

3. Remove the chicken from the refrigerator, discarding the marinade, and thread the pre-soaked skewers through the strips in two places, a third of the distance from each end.

4. Before grilling, place a folded piece of foil directly on the grill under the exposed wood of the skewers to help prevent burning. Brush the chicken with butter and grill over Direct High heat until fully cooked – about 4 minutes – turning once halfway through the grilling time.

5. To serve, arrange on a platter and serve with a favourite relish or chutney.

Vera Cruz Mini Fish Burritos

Gas Direct Medium Heat / **Weber® Q™** Direct Medium Heat / **Charcoal** Direct
Prep time 15 minutes + 40 minutes chilling / **Grilling time** 11 to 14 minutes / **Makes** 8

**8 monkfish fillets, each
weighing about 75g and
2.5cm thick**
Vegetable oil, for brushing
**8 soft flour tortillas 15cm
across**

For the paste:
115ml tomato ketchup
3 tablespoons orange juice
1 tablespoon soy sauce
**3 teaspoons Mexican spice
blend (to include chilli
powder, cumin and
coriander)**

To serve:
**8 tablespoons of Grilled
Tomato Confit Salsa
(see page 20)**
**8 tablespoons soured cream
(optional)**
15g fresh coriander leaves

1. To prepare the paste: in a small bowl, combine the ketchup, orange juice and soy sauce. Add the spices and stir into a smooth paste.

2. Rinse the monkfish under cold running water and pat dry with kitchen paper, then rub the paste all over. Place the fillets in a shallow dish, cover and refrigerate for 40 minutes.

3. Remove the fish from the refrigerator and allow to sit at room temperature for 10 minutes, then brush with oil.

4. Grill over Direct Medium heat until fully cooked, 8 to 10 minutes, turning once halfway through.

5. Meanwhile, separate the tortillas and divide them between two foil packages. Grill over Direct Medium heat for 3 to 4 minutes to warm through.

6. To serve, roll a tablespoon of salsa on the inside of each warm tortilla and place a monkfish fillet in the centre. A dollop of soured cream may be added, if desired. Sprinkle some fresh coriander over the top and wrap into small parcels.

Chipotle-laced Pork Brochettes

Gas Direct High Heat / **Weber® Q™** Direct High Heat / **Charcoal** Direct
Prep time 15 minutes + overnight marinating / **Grilling time** 11 to 14 minutes / **Makes** 8

900g pork tenderloin
Vegetable oil, for brushing
**16 soft flour tortillas 15cm
across**
**225ml soured cream with
chives, to serve**

For the marinade:
**½ teaspoon chipotle powder
(or chilli powder if not
available)**
1 teaspoon ground cumin
4 garlic cloves, crushed
2 tablespoons dried oregano
6 tablespoons orange juice
¼ teaspoon salt

TIP
Chipotle powder
is made from
smoky, hot
jalapeño
peppers.

1. To make the marinade: combine all the ingredients in a medium bowl and whisk to a thin paste. Leave to rest at room temperature while the pork is prepared.

2. Cut the pork into 2cm cubes. Lay the cubes in a large shallow dish, pour over the marinade and toss the meat until the surfaces are fully coated. Cover with clingfilm and refrigerate overnight.

3. When ready to grill, drain the pork and discard the marinade. Thread the pork cubes on to 8 metal skewers, then brush the surfaces with the oil.

4. Grill over Direct High heat until fully cooked, 8 to 10 minutes, or 2 to 3 minutes each side.

5. Meanwhile, separate the tortillas and divide them between four foil packages. Grill over Direct High heat for 3 to 4 minutes to warm them.

6. To serve, give each person a brochette and 2 warm tortillas on a plate. The pork can be drawn off the skewer, with the tortilla wrapped around the meat. A dollop of soured cream is recommended as an accompaniment.

Baby Beef Burritos

Gas Direct Medium Heat / **Weber® Q™** Direct Medium Heat / **Charcoal** Direct
Prep time 10 minutes + 4 hours marinating / **Grilling time** 10 to 12 minutes / **Makes** 8

**675g flank steak, trimmed
of fat**
Vegetable oil, for brushing
¼ teaspoon coarse sea salt
**8 soft flour tortillas 15cm
across**
**15g fresh coriander leaves,
to serve**
**Salsa and soured cream,
to serve**

For the paste:
115ml tomato ketchup
6 tablespoons lime juice
5 garlic cloves, crushed
1 teaspoon chilli powder
**¼ teaspoon ground
cinnamon**

1. To prepare the paste: in a small bowl, combine the ketchup and lime juice. Add the garlic and spices, then stir into a smooth paste. Leave to rest at room temperature while preparing the meat.

2. Score a cross-hatch pattern on both sides of the steak to stop it curling on the grill, then rub over the paste using a brush. Put the steak in a shallow dish, cover and refrigerate for 4 hours.

3. Remove the steak from the refrigerator and allow to sit at room temperature for 10 minutes, then brush with oil. Grill over Direct Medium heat until medium rare, 8 to 10 minutes, turning once halfway through.

4. Transfer the steak to a chopping board, sprinkle with salt and loosely cover with foil. While the beef is resting separate the tortillas and divide them between two foil packages. Grill over Direct Medium heat for 3 to 4 minutes to warm through.

5. After the beef has rested for 5 minutes slice it paper-thin at a 45-degree angle along the broadest side. Transfer the slices to a platter.

6. To serve, place a mound of beef in the centre of each warm tortilla. Sprinkle some fresh coriander over the top and wrap into small parcels. Serve with salsa and a dollop of soured cream.

TIP

Always buy coriander with the roots attached for optimum flavour. The roots can also be frozen and kept for use in stocks and stews.

Petite Mixed Grill Kebabs

Gas Direct Medium Heat / **Weber® Q™** Direct Medium Heat / **Charcoal** Direct
Prep time 15 minutes + overnight marinating / **Grilling time** 10 to 12 minutes / **Makes** 8

450g beef tenderloin
450g loin of veal
3 tablespoons melted
butter, for basting
¼ teaspoon coarse sea salt
8 Middle Eastern flatbreads
or soft tortillas

For the marinade:
8 garlic cloves, crushed
with 1 tablespoon coarse
sea salt
115ml dry sherry
2 teaspoons chilli sauce
2 tablespoons fresh
rosemary, finely chopped

1. To prepare the marinade: combine all the ingredients in a medium bowl and stir until well combined. Leave to rest at room temperature while preparing the meat.

2. Cut the beef and veal into 2.5cm cubes. Lay them in a large shallow dish, pour over the marinade and toss the meat until the surfaces are fully coated. Cover with clingfilm and refrigerate overnight.

3. When ready to grill, drain the meat and discard the marinade. Alternately thread the beef and veal cubes on to 8 metal skewers and brush with butter.

4. Grill the meat over Direct Medium heat until fully cooked, 8 to 10 minutes for medium rare to medium, turning once halfway through. Brush with butter two or three times while cooking.

5. Remove from the grill, transfer to a serving platter and sprinkle salt over the top. Cover loosely with foil and allow to rest for 5 minutes.

6. Meanwhile, divide the flatbreads between two foil packages and grill over Direct Medium heat for 3 to 4 minutes to warm through.

7. To serve, offer each person a piece of flatbread with which to take the meat from the skewer.

TIP

This recipe is derived from the Brazilian barbecue known as *Churascaria*, which consists of meat served on long metal skewers.

Grilled Tomato Confit Salsa

Gas Indirect Medium Heat / **Weber® Q™** Direct Low Heat / **Charcoal** Indirect
Prep time 20 minutes / **Grilling time** 20 minutes / **Serves** 4

10 firm ripe plum or Roma tomatoes, sliced in half
Extra-virgin olive oil
50g red onion, finely chopped
3 garlic cloves, crushed
1 jalapeño chilli, deseeded and finely chopped
1 tablespoon lime juice
¼ teaspoon ground cumin
25g fresh coriander leaves, to serve
¼ teaspoon coarse sea salt

1. Brush the tomato halves with oil and place them, skin side down, over Indirect Medium heat (or Direct Low heat on the Weber® Q™ grill) and grill for 20 minutes. Gently transfer them to a non-metallic bowl. Remove and discard the outer skin. Leave to rest at room temperature for 20 minutes, or until cooled.

2. Drain and discard the excess liquid from the tomatoes, then snip them into shreds with kitchen scissors. Add the remaining ingredients, except the salt to the bowl and stir with a wooden spoon.

3. To serve, add extra salt to taste, stir and transfer to a ceramic serving bowl. Sprinkle coriander over the top and serve as a condiment or as a dip to accompany crispy corn chips.

Mexican Wave

1 part tequila
½ part crème de cassis
½ part sugar syrup
Ginger ale
Lime slices, to garnish

Shake the tequila, crème de cassis and sugar syrup in a cocktail shaker with cracked ice. Strain into an old-fashioned glass, top up with ginger ale, and mix with a glass swizzle stick. Float a few lime slices on top to garnish.

Pina Colada

2 parts golden, white or dark rum
3 parts pineapple juice or ½ cup diced
pineapple pieces
2 dashes of Angostura bitters (optional)
1 part coconut cream or fresh
coconut milk
½ part single cream
1 pineapple wedge and 1 maraschino
cherry, to garnish

Combine all ingredients with four or five ice cubes in a blender. Blend until smooth. Pour into a large goblet or Boston glass. Garnish with a large wedge of pineapple and a maraschino cherry.

Margarita

Fine sea salt
1½ parts gold tequila
1 part freshly squeezed lime juice
1 part Cointreau
1 lime wedge, to garnish

Salt the rim of a champagne saucer. Shake all of the liquid ingredients and strain into the glass. Garnish with a lime wedge on the rim of the glass.

Mai Tai

1 part light rum
½ part dark rum
1 part orange juice
1 part apricot brandy
½ part tequila
½ part Cointreau or triple sec
2 dashes of grenadine
1 Dash of Amaretto or orgeat
1 Dash of Angostura bitters
Slices of orange, lemon and lime and
   1 sprig of mint, to garnish

Shake the ingredients vigorously in a cocktail shaker with
cracked ice. Strain into an old-fashioned glass or large goblet,
half-filled with crushed ice. Garnish with slices of orange, lemon
and lime, a maraschino cherry and a sprig of mint.

Bamboozle
(non-alcoholic)

3 parts guava juice
2 parts orange juice
2 parts passion fruit juice
1 dash of freshly squeezed lime juice
Soda water (optional)
1 sprig of bamboo, to garnish

Combine the juices with cracked ice in a cocktail shaker.
Shake vigorously. Strain into a highball glass, half-filled with
crushed ice. Top up with a little soda water if desired.
Garnish with a sprig of bamboo.

Caribbean Champagne Cocktail

¼ **part light rum**
¼ **part crème de banane**
1 dash of Angostura bitters
Chilled champagne
2 slices of banana, 1 maraschino cherry
   and 1 pineapple leaf, to garnish

Pour the rum, crème de banane and
Angostura bitters into a champagne flute. Top
with champagne and stir gently with a glass
rod. Garnish with slices of banana, a
maraschino cherry and a pineapple leaf.

Windward Island

1 part golden rum
½ **part Tia Maria**
Cola
Orange slices, to garnish

Shake the rum and Tia Maria vigorously in a cocktail
shaker with cracked ice. Strain into an old-fashioned
glass almost filled with ice cubes. Top up with cola
and garnish with orange slices.

CHAPTER TWO

Pan-Asian

Red Coconut Curry Lamb Kebabs

Gas Indirect Medium Heat / **Weber® Q™** Direct Low Heat / **Charcoal** Indirect
Prep time 25 minutes + overnight marinating / **Grilling time** 6 to 8 minutes / **Makes** 16

**900g boneless leg of lamb,
    trimmed of fat**
¼ teaspoon salt
**16 large outer leaves of
    iceberg lettuce, to serve**
**3 tablespoons fresh mint,
    finely chopped, to serve**

For the marinade:
2 tablespoons peanut oil
3 garlic cloves, crushed
**1 teaspoon red curry paste
    (or 1 tablespoon hot
    curry powder)**
2 tablespoons soy sauce
225ml coconut milk
**Salt and freshly ground
    black pepper**

1. To make the marinade: heat the oil in a pan over a medium heat. Add the garlic and stir with a wooden spoon for 3 minutes, or until softened. Add the curry paste and soy sauce and cook for 2 minutes. Pour in the coconut milk, stir, season to taste and bring to the boil. Reduce the heat and set aside to cool at room temperature.

2. Cut the lamb into 2.5cm cubes and lay them in a large shallow dish. Pour over the marinade and toss until the meat is fully coated. Cover with clingfilm and refrigerate overnight.

3. When ready to grill, drain the lamb cubes, discarding the marinade, and thread them on to 8 metal skewers.

4. Grill over Indirect Medium heat (or Direct Low heat on the Weber® Q™ grill) until fully cooked, 6 to 8 minutes for medium rare to medium, turning once halfway through. Brush surfaces with butter two or three times while cooking.

5. To serve, remove the lamb from the skewers and place several chunks of meat in the lettuce leaves and fold to make a wrap.

Mini Salmon Rice Burgers

Gas Direct High Heat / **Weber® Q™** Direct High Heat / **Charcoal** Direct
Prep time 25 minutes / **Grilling time** 8 to 10 minutes / **Makes** 8

**50g raw sushi rice to make
175g cooked rice (follow
instructions on packet)**
**450g salmon fillet, skinned
and slightly frozen**
**6 tablespoons teriyaki
sauce**
**1 teaspoon powdered
wasabi (or dry yellow
mustard powder)**
2 garlic cloves, crushed
**3 tablespoons fresh root
ginger, finely chopped**
Vegetable oil, for brushing
¼ teaspoon salt

1. To make the burgers: place the cooked sushi rice in a medium bowl and leave at room temperature. Remove the slightly frozen salmon from the freezer and rinse under cold running water. Check for remaining bones and pat the salmon dry with kitchen paper. Place the salmon on a chopping board and cut it into 6mm cubes before transferring to a medium bowl.

2. Whisk the teriyaki sauce and mustard to a thin paste in a small bowl, then add the garlic, ginger and salt. Reserve 3 tablespoons of this mixture for glazing. Pour the remainder over the salmon and stir.

3. Add the cooked rice to the salmon and mix evenly by hand. Form into eight small, round patties 2.5cm thick. Transfer to a plate lined with greaseproof paper.

4. Lightly brush both sides of the burgers with oil, then grill over Direct High heat until medium rare, 8 to 10 minutes, brushing with the reserved glaze and turning once halfway through. Remove from the heat and serve warm.

1 part gin
1 part orange juice
1 orange slice, to garnish

Orange Blossom

Shake ingredients vigorously in a cocktail shaker with cracked ice. Strain into a chilled old-fashioned glass and serve straight up. Garnish with a slice of orange.

Spiced Skewered Prawns (see p. 48/49)

Gas Direct High Heat / **Weber® Q™** Direct High Heat / **Charcoal** Direct
Prep time 15 minutes + 1 hour marinating / **Grilling time** 4 to 6 minutes / **Makes** 8

900g king prawns, shelled with tails
3 tablespoons melted butter, for basting
25g fresh coriander, coarsely chopped, to serve
8 wooden skewers soaked in cold water for 30 minutes

For the marinade:
400ml coconut milk
1 teaspoon sambal ulek (or chilli sauce)
2 garlic cloves, crushed

For the dipping sauce:
225g fresh pineapple, chopped, and juices reserved
2 tablespoons ketjap manis (or equal amounts of molasses and soy sauce if not available)
2 tablespoons peanut oil
1 tablespoon fresh root ginger, crushed

1. To prepare the marinade: in a small bowl combine all the ingredients and stir well. Leave to rest until needed.

2. After rinsing the prawns, pat them dry with kitchen paper and place in a shallow dish. Pour the marinade over the top and toss gently. Cover with clingfilm and refrigerate for 1 hour.

3. To make the dipping sauce: put the pineapple plus juice and the ketjap manis in a blender or food processor and process until completely smooth. Heat the oil in a small saucepan, then sauté the ginger until it just begins to brown. Add the processed liquid, stir and bring to the boil. Reduce the heat and simmer for 3 minutes, or until it thickens slightly. Pour into a small bowl and allow to rest until ready to serve.

4. Drain the prawns from the marinade and divide them between the pre-soaked skewers, piercing each one through the flesh near to the head and again near to the tail.

5. Grill over Direct High heat for 4 to 6 minutes until the flesh is opaque. Brush with the melted butter and turn once halfway through the grilling time.

6. To serve, sprinkle the skewers with coriander and serve with a bowl of the dipping sauce.

Seared Tuna
with Wasabi Mayonnaise

Gas Direct High Heat / **Weber® Q™** Direct High Heat / **Charcoal** Direct
Prep time 15 minutes + 1 hour marinating / **Grilling time** 8 to 10 minutes / **Makes** 8

8 sushi-quality tuna steaks, each weighing about 115g and 2.5cm thick
Vegetable oil, for brushing

For the mayonnaise:
1 teaspoon powdered wasabi (or dry yellow mustard powder)
1 teaspoon cold water
225ml mayonnaise

For the marinade:
8 tablespoons soy sauce
2 tablespoons light sesame oil
Salt and freshly ground black pepper
4 garlic cloves, crushed
2 tablespoons fresh root ginger, finely chopped

1. To make the mayonnaise: whisk the wasabi and water together into a paste. Add the mayonnaise and stir well. Cover and refrigerate until required.

2. To make the marinade: whisk the soy sauce and sesame oil together in a small bowl until evenly combined, then add the seasoning, garlic and ginger. Stir well.

3. Rinse the tuna under cold running water, pat dry with kitchen paper and slice to specified weight and thickness.

4. Place the steaks in a shallow dish, pour over the marinade and turn the fish several times. Cover with clingfilm and refrigerate for 1 hour.

5. Remove the tuna from the refrigerator and leave to stand at room temperature for 10 minutes. Drain, reserving the marinade, and lightly brush both sides of the fish with oil. Grill over Direct High heat until medium rare, 8 to 10 minutes, brushing with the reserved marinade and turning once halfway through.

6. Serve the tuna with a dollop of wasabi mayonnaise and a coleslaw of fennel, pepper and cabbage if desired.

Hoisin-style Beef Strips

Gas Direct High Heat / **Weber® Q™** Direct High Heat / **Charcoal** Direct
Prep time 20 minutes + overnight marinating / **Grilling time** 4 minutes / **Makes** 8

**675g flank steak, cleaned
and trimmed of fat
50g spring onion, white and
trimmed green parts,
finely chopped, to serve**

For the marinade:
**1 small red chilli, deseeded
and finely chopped
225ml hoisin sauce
50ml rice wine vinegar**

For the glaze:
**3 tablespoons butter
3 tablespoons hoisin sauce**

1. To prepare the marinade: in a large shallow dish, combine the ingredients and stir well.

2. Cut the steak into 6mm thick slices and then strips of 2 x 13cm at a 45-degree angle. Place in a shallow dish, pour over the marinade and toss the steak until well coated. Cover with clingfilm and refrigerate overnight.

3. Remove the steak from the refrigerator, discarding the marinade, and thread the strips on to eight 20-cm long metal skewers in a weaving fashion. When the skewer is full, the strip will resemble a concertina.

4. To make the glaze: melt the butter in a saucepan and add the hoisin sauce, stirring until well combined.

5. Grill the beef over Direct High heat until fully cooked – about 4 minutes. Brush the surfaces with the glaze and turn once halfway through the grilling time.

6. To serve, arrange the skewers on a serving platter and sprinkle the chopped spring onion over the top.

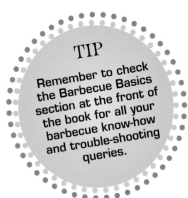

TIP
Remember to check the Barbecue Basics section at the front of the book for all your barbecue know-how and trouble-shooting queries.

Five-spice Baby Spareribs

Gas Indirect Medium + Direct Low Heat / **Weber® Q™** Direct Medium + Low Heat / **Charcoal** Indirect + Direct / **Prep time** 5 minutes + marinating / **Grilling time** 2 hours / **Serves** 8

2.5kg baby back spare ribs (4 slabs), membrane removed
3 garlic cloves, pressed
2 tablespoons balsamic vinegar
2 tablespoons Chinese five-spice powder
¼ teaspoon salt

For the marinade:
225ml ketjap manis (or equal amounts of molasses and soy sauce)
50ml orange juice
1 teaspoon sambal ulek (or chilli sauce)
4 lime leaves

1. Stir the garlic and vinegar with the five-spice powder, and rub in to the ribs. Lay them flat on a baking sheet.

2. Place the slabs on the grill, flesh side up and grill over Indirect Medium heat for 1½ hours.

3. If you are using the Weber® Q™ grill or a charcoal grill, fold a sheet of aluminium foil in half to just fit over the cooking grate (leaving a little space all the way round). Brush the top of the foil with vegetable oil and place the ribs on top. Cook over Direct Medium heat for 1½ hours.

4. To make the marinade: combine all the ingredients in a medium bowl and stir until well mixed. Leave to stand at room temperature until the ribs have completed their indirect cooking phase.

5. Remove the ribs from the grill and return to the baking sheet. Pour two-thirds of the marinade over the ribs and brush it over all surfaces. Leave to rest at room temperature for 15 minutes.

6. Place the ribs on the grill, flesh side down, and cook over Direct Low heat for 15 minutes, turning once, and brushing with the reserved marinade in the final 10 minutes cooking time.

7. Slice the ribs into single or double-rib portions before serving.

TIP

It may be necessary to add additional briquettes to the charcoal barbecue halfway through slow-cooking recipes.

Javanese-style Chicken Satay

Gas Direct High Heat / **Weber® Q™** Direct High Heat / **Charcoal** Direct
Prep time 25 minutes + 1 hour marinating / **Grilling time** 4 minutes / **Makes** 8

1 tablespoon sambal ulek (or chilli sauce)
1 tablespoon olive oil
675g skinless chicken breast
3 tablespoons melted butter, for basting
25g fresh coriander, finely chopped, to serve
Several wooden skewers soaked in cold water for 30 minutes

For the dipping sauce:
4 tablespoons peanut butter
2 tablespoons kejap manis (or equal amounts of molasses and soy sauce)
175ml coconut milk

TIP
Never spray or brush oil directly on to a hot cooking grate – brush the food with oil before cooking instead.

1. Place the sambal ulek (or chilli sauce) and olive oil in a small bowl and stir well.

2. Rinse the chicken thoroughly under cold running water, pat dry with kitchen paper and cut into 2.5 x 10cm strips. Place in a shallow dish, pour over the marinade and toss until fully coated. Cover with clingfilm and refrigerate for 1 hour.

3. To make the dipping sauce: put all the ingredients in a medium saucepan and bring to the boil over a medium heat. Reduce the heat to low, stir and simmer for 10 minutes, or until a smooth, pourable consistency is reached. Remove from the heat.

4. Remove the chicken from the refrigerator and drain and discard the marinade. Thread the presoaked skewers through the chicken strips in two places, a third of the distance from each end.

5. Before grilling the satays, place a folded piece of foil directly on the grill under the exposed wood of the skewers to help prevent burning. Grill over Direct High heat until fully cooked – about 4 minutes. Brush surfaces with butter and turn once halfway through the grilling time.

6. Sprinkle the satays with coriander before serving with the dipping sauce.

Pink Lady

2 parts sake
1 part vodka
½ part gin
½ part Cointreau or triple sec
1 maraschino cherry, to garnish

Combine the ingredients with cracked ice in a mixing flass. Stir and strain into a cocktail glass. Serve straight up and garnish with a maraschino cherry.

Stinger

2 parts brandy
2 parts white crème de menthe
1 part freshly squeezed lime juice
1 lime twist, to garnish

Shake the ingredients vigorously in a cocktail shaker with cracked ice. Strain into a chilled highball glass and serve straight up with a twist of lime.

Sloe Gin Fizz

3 parts sloe gin
2 parts sweet vermouth
1 part freshly squeezed lemon juice
Soda water

Shake the gin, vermouth and lemon juice vigorously in a cocktail shaker with cracked ice. Strain into a highball glass. Add ice cubes and fill the glass with soda water.

Thai Tiger

1 part lemon grass and ginger syrup
2 parts fresh coconut juice (optional)
1 part vodka
1 small chilli, deseeded and sliced
1½ parts freshly squeezed lime juice
Lemonade
1 lemon grass stick, 1 sliver of chilli and
1 lime wedge, to garnish

Combine the flavoured syrup, coconut juice (if using), vodka, sliced chilli and lime juice in a cocktail shaker with cracked ice. Shake well. Strain into a highball glass half-filled with crushed ice. Top up with lemonade. Garnish with a stick of lemongrass, a sliver of chilli and a slender wedge of lime.

Lemon grass and ginger syrup:
Add 1 stick of crushed lemon grass, a 2.5cm piece of peeled fresh root ginger cut into slivers, and one or two lime leaves to a pan containing 2 parts granulated sugar and 1 part water. Stir over a gentle heat then bring to the boil for 3 to 5 minutes. The longer you boil it, the more concentrated it will become. Cool, then pour into a bottle and refrigerate until needed.

CHAPTER THREE

American

Granny Smith Apple Blues

Gas Direct Medium Heat / **Weber® Q™** Direct Medium Heat / **Charcoal** Direct
Prep time 15 minutes / **Grilling time** 4 minutes / **Serves** 8

**4 Granny Smith apples,
   peeled, halved and cored**
**225g Gorgonzola,
   refrigerated firm**

For the marinade:
115ml orange juice
2 tablespoons vegetable oil
**2 tablespoons orange
   marmalade**

1. To make the marinade: whisk all the ingredients together in a shallow dish.

2. To prepare the apples: slice the apple halves into wedges about 1.5cm thick. Dredge them through the marinade or brush them with it, then put them on a plate.

3. Grill immediately over Direct Medium heat for 4 minutes until browned, turning only once. Brush the surfaces with the marinade while grilling.

4. Slice the Gorgonzola into similar thickness slices as the apple. To serve, transfer to a platter and set a thin slice of Gorgonzola to cover each piece of grilled apple. Pass the platter round as the cheese begins to melt, with shelled walnuts as an accompaniment.

Applejack

1 part apple brandy
1 part grapefruit juice
Dash of grenadine
1 lemon twist, to garnish

Stir or shake the ingredients with cracked ice. Strain into a cocktail glass filled with crushed ice and serve with a twist of lemon.

Creole Gulf Prawns

Gas Direct High Heat / **Weber® Q™** Direct High Heat / **Charcoal** Direct
Prep time 25 minutes + 1 hour marinating / **Grilling time** 6 to 8 minutes / **Serves** 8

**2 teaspoons cayenne
    pepper**
4 tablespoons olive oil
**675 to 900g king prawns,
    shelled with tails and
    deveined**
**Several wooden skewers
    soaked in cold water for
    30 minutes**

For the Creole sauce:
3 tablespoons olive oil
**1 medium onion, finely
    chopped**
3 garlic cloves, crushed
**1 jalapeño chilli, deseeded
    and finely chopped**
**2 tablespoons Mexican
    spice blend (to include
    oregano and cumin)**
**400g can chopped
    tomatoes with liquid**
1 teaspoon sea salt

1. Rinse the prawns thoroughly under cold running water and pat dry with kitchen paper.

2. In a small bowl, stir the cayenne pepper and oil together until well combined. Place the prawns in a shallow dish and pour the cayenne mixture over the prawns, then toss by hand, working the mixture into the flesh of the prawns. Cover with clingfilm and refrigerate for 1 hour.

3. To make the sauce: heat the oil in a medium saucepan over a medium heat. Add the garlic and onion and sauté until translucent – 3 to 4 minutes. Add the tomato purée, jalapeño chilli and spice blend. Stir for 1 minute, then add the tomatoes and increase the heat to high. Bring to the boil and reduce for 5 minutes. Season with salt.

4. Divide the prawns between the presoaked skewers, piercing each one near the head and again near the tail. Grill over Direct High heat for 6 to 8 minutes until the flesh is opaque, turning once halfway through.

5. To serve, pour the warm Creole sauce into a bowl and arrange the skewered prawns around it.

Grilled Smoked Salmon Roll-ups

Gas Direct High Heat / **Weber® Q™** Direct High Heat / **Charcoal** Direct
Prep time 10 minutes / **Grilling time** 4 minutes / **Makes** 16

**8 soft flour tortillas
15 to 20cm across
225g thinly sliced smoked
salmon
8 fresh dill sprigs, plus
extra to garnish
Vegetable oil, for brushing
Lemon wedges, to garnish
Several wooden skewers
soaked in cold water for
30 minutes**

For the filling:
**175g cream cheese
1 small sweet red onion,
finely chopped
1 teaspoon lemon juice
1 teaspoon fresh cracked
black pepper**

1. To prepare the filling: in a small bowl mix all the ingredients until they are evenly combined.

2. To make the roll-ups: lay each piece of tortilla on a clean work surface. Spread a thin, even layer of the filling over the top, then lay a piece of smoked salmon on top. Put a sprig of dill on the centre of the salmon. Roll up the tortilla into a long sausage.

3. Working with two roll-ups at a time, pierce one presoaked skewer through one and then the other roll-up, 5cm from the ends. Repeat on the other side. Continue with the three other pairs.

4. Brush the roll-ups lightly with oil. Place each set of roll-ups over Direct High heat, just long enough to warm and score the tortilla, 4 minutes, turning once halfway through the grilling time.

5. To serve, carefully remove the skewers. Slice each roll-up on a chopping board into halves or thirds. Arrange on a platter and garnish with extra dill and lemon wedges.

Mini Crab Cakes

Gas Direct Medium Heat / **Weber® Q™** Direct Medium Heat / **Charcoal** Direct
Prep time 20 minutes / **Grilling time** 8 to 10 minutes / **Makes** 8

900g crab meat
2 tablespoons lemon juice
900g mashed potatoes at room temperature
6 egg whites
2 tablespoons Dijon mustard
½ teaspoon cayenne pepper
1 tablespoon coarse sea salt
Freshly ground black pepper
115g melted butter, for basting
8 lemon wedges, to serve
Fresh dill sprigs, to garnish

1. To prepare the crab cakes: check through the crab meat for any bits of shell or cartilage and discard. Toss in lemon juice and set aside.

2. Combine all the remaining ingredients apart from the butter in a large bowl. Gently fold in the crab meat and mix until evenly distributed. Divide the mixture into twenty-four equal parts. Wet your hands and form into small patties 1.5cm thick. To avoid sticking, place the patties on a sheet of greaseproof paper over a baking sheet.

3. Grill the crab cakes over Direct Medium heat until fully cooked, about 8 to 10 minutes. Brush with butter and turn once halfway through the grilling time.

4. To serve, transfer directly to a platter and garnish with lemon wedges and dill sprigs.

Harvey Wallbanger

4 parts orange juice
2 parts vodka
½ part Galliano
Orange slices, to garnish

Pour the orange juice and the vodka into a highball glass filled with ice. Stir, and then float the Galliano on the top. Garnish with orange slices.

Buffalo Chicken Wings

Gas Indirect Medium Heat / **Weber® Q™** Direct Low Heat / **Charcoal** Indirect
Prep time 25 minutes + 3 hours marinating / **Grilling time** 30 minutes / **Serves** 8

675g skinless chicken wings

For the marinade:
115g butter
3 garlic cloves, crushed
**1 tablespoon fresh root
  ginger, finely chopped**
2 tablespoons lime juice
2 tablespoons soy sauce
**2 teaspoons sambal ulek
  (or chilli sauce if not
  available)**

For the sauce:
115g blue cheese
225ml light mayonnaise
**½ teaspoon freshly ground
  black pepper**

1. To prepare the marinade: in a small saucepan over a medium heat melt half the butter. Add the garlic and ginger and sauté for 2 to 3 minutes, or until translucent. Add the lime juice, soy sauce and sambal ulek, then bring to the boil. Add the remaining butter and stir until it has melted. Remove from the heat and leave to cool at room temperature.

2. Rinse the chicken thoroughly under cold running water and pat dry with kitchen paper. Cut the segments of each wing at each joint and discard the bony tip (or reserve for use in stock). Pour the marinade over the chicken and toss until fully coated. Cover with clingfilm and refrigerate for 3 hours.

3. To make the sauce: in a medium bowl mash the cheese with a fork. Add the mayonnaise and pepper, and beat well until smooth. Cover with clingfilm and refrigerate until just before serving the chicken.

4. Remove the chicken from the refrigerator and discard the marinade. Grill the chicken over Indirect Medium heat (or Direct Low heat on the Weber® Q™) until fully cooked – about 30 minutes. Turn only once halfway through the grilling time.

5. To serve, place the chicken in a large serving platter and take to the table. Serve the sauce in a small bowl for guests to take from separately.

Columbia Honey Mustard Pork Kebabs

Gas Direct High Heat / **Weber® Q™** Direct High Heat / **Charcoal** Direct
Prep time 15 minutes + overnight marinating / **Grilling time** 10 to 12 minutes / **Makes** 8

900g pork tenderloin
Vegetable oil, for brushing
¼ teaspoon coarse sea salt
8 mini pitta breads
1 medium red onion, finely sliced in rings and lime wedges, to garnish

For the marinade:
115ml yellow mustard
2 tablespoons white wine vinegar
3 tablespoons light runny honey
¼ teaspoon cayenne pepper

TIP

Wash your hands thoroughly with warm, soapy water before starting any meal preparation and after handling fresh meat, fish or poultry.

1. To make the marinade: combine all the ingredients in a medium bowl and stir to make a smooth sauce. Leave at room temperature until the pork is ready to marinate.

2. Cut the pork into 2cm cubes. Lay them in a large shallow dish, pour over the marinade and toss the meat until the surfaces are fully coated. Cover with clingfilm and refrigerate overnight.

3. When ready to grill, drain the pork and discard the marinade. Thread on to eight 20cm long metal skewers through the centre of each cube and brush the surfaces with oil.

4. Grill the pork over Direct High heat until fully cooked, 6 to 8 minutes, or 2 to 3 minutes each side. Sprinkle salt over the top.

5. Meanwhile, snip a thin layer off the top of each pitta bread so it will be easier to fill them. Divide them between four foil packages, or brush them with oil and place directly on the cooking grate and grill over Direct High heat for 4 minutes to warm them.

6. To serve, divide the meat from each skewer into two pitta breads. Place a few onion slices over the pork and garnish with lime wedges.

Cocktail Butter Burgers (see p. 62/63)

Gas Direct Medium Heat / **Weber® Q™** Direct Medium Heat / **Charcoal** Direct
Prep time 20 minutes + 1 hour refrigerating / **Grilling time** 8 to 10 minutes / **Makes** 8

**450g each freshly minced
chuck and sirloin steak or
900g lean minced beef**
¼ teaspoon coarse sea salt
Freshly ground black pepper
**3 tablespoons melted
butter**
8 soft rolls, sliced in half

For the seasoned butter:
**6 tablespoons melted
butter**
**2 tablespoons tomato
ketchup**
**1 teaspoon Worcestershire
sauce**
3 dashes Tabasco sauce

1. To prepare the butter: combine all the ingredients in a small plastic container. Stir until well combined, then cover and refrigerate for 1 hour.

2. Place the minced beef in a mixing bowl and season. Divide into eight equal parts and shape into balls. Flatten into patties and, with your thumb, make a hollow in the top of each one.

3. Remove the seasoned butter from the refrigerator. Using a teaspoon, scoop an eighth of it into the hollow at the top of each patty. Press the meat up over the hollow, enclosing the butter, and form into a patty 2cm thick.

4. Transfer to a plate lined with greaseproof paper to prevent sticking. Grill the burgers over Direct Medium heat for 8 to 10 minutes for medium to medium-well done. Turn only once halfway through the cooking time.

5. Brush the cut side of the rolls with a little melted butter. For the last 2 minutes of the burgers cooking time, place the split rolls, cut-side down, around the outside of the barbecue.

6. To serve, put the burgers in the rolls on a platter and garnish with salad, tomato and red onion rings. You could offer tomato ketchup or spicy mayonnaise in addition to the standard accompaniments.

TIP
While preparing the burgers, handle them as little as possible to ensure a coarser and juicier texture.

Mini Jacket Potatoes
with Cheddar Cheese & Chives

Gas Indirect Medium Heat / **Weber® Q™** Direct Low Heat / **Charcoal** Indirect
Prep time 15 minutes / **Grilling time** 45 minutes / **Serves** 4

**4 small potatoes, scrubbed,
   each weighing about 75g**
1 tablespoon olive oil
¼ teaspoon sea salt

For the filling:
25g butter
**50g Cheddar cheese, finely
   grated**
4 tablespoons soured cream
**2 tablespoons freshly
   snipped chives**
¼ teaspoon cayenne pepper
Freshly ground black pepper

1. Pierce the potatoes with a fork and pack neatly in a foil container suitable for cooking on the barbecue (the Weber small drip pan is ideal). Drizzle with olive oil and sprinkle with sea salt. Turn so the potatoes are nicely coated.

2. Cook on the barbecue over Indirect Medium heat (or Direct Low heat on the Weber® Q™) for about 45 minutes or until the potatoes are very tender. Turn a couple of times so they are evenly browned.

3. Cut the potatoes in half, scoop out the flesh and mix this with the butter and cheese. Then pile the filling back into the potato skins, add a dollop of soured cream, a scattering of chives, a sprinkling of cayenne pepper and a couple of twists of black pepper.

TIP
Grills radiate a lot of heat, so always keep the grill at least 3m from any combustible materials, including the house, garage, fences etc. Never use a grill indoors or under a covered patio.

75

Sea Mist

3 parts cranberry and raspberry juice
3 parts pink grapefruit juice
2 parts vodka
Slices of lime and lemon frozen in ice cubes

Shake the fruit juices and vodka
thoroughly in a cocktail shaker with
cracked ice. Strain into a highball glass
filled with decorated ice cubes.

Cosmopolitan

1½ parts lemon-flavoured vodka
1 part triple sec
1 dash freshly squeezed lime juice
1 part cranberry juice
1 flamed orange twist, to garnish

Shake all of the liquid ingredients with ice and
strain into a chilled Martini glass. Cut a small oval
of peel from an orange, leaving a little pith intact.
Pinch the oval skin-side out over a flame. Squeeze
it firmly so that the oil is released – it will ignite to
give you an impressive flair, with a fantastic aroma
– and then drop it in the drink.

Long Island Iced Tea

½ **part golden rum**
½ **part gin**
½ **part vodka**
½ **part tequila**
½ **part Cointreau or triple sec**
½ **part sugar syrup**
1 part freshly squeezed lime juice
Cola
Lime wedges, to garnish

Combine all the ingredients, except the cola, in a cocktail shaker with cracked ice. Shake well. Strain into a highball glass half-filled with ice. Top up with a dash of cola and garnish with a wedge of lime.

Daiquiri

3 parts light rum
1 part freshly squeezed lime juice
½ **teaspoon sugar syrup**
**1 lime slice and 1 maraschino
  cherry, to garnish**

Shake the ingredients in a shaker with cracked ice. Strain into a chilled cocktail glass and serve. Garnish with a slice of lime and a maraschino cherry.

Dry Martini

4 parts gin
1 part dry vermouth
1 stoned green olive, to garnish

Stir ingredients with cracked ice in a mixing glass. Strain into a chilled cocktail glass and serve straight up. Garnish with a green olive.

Planters' Punch

3 parts Jamaican rum
1 part freshly squeezed lime juice
1 teaspoon sugar
1 dash of Angostura bitters
Soda water
1 maraschino cherry, 1 pineapple cube,
  1 slice of orange and 1 sprig of mint,
  to garnish

Shake the rum, lime juice, sugar and bitters in a cocktail shaker with cracked ice. Strain into a highball glass half-filled with crushed ice. Top up with soda water. Garnish with a maraschino cherry, a cube of pineapple, a slice of orange and a sprig of mint.

CHAPTER FOUR

Med Fusion

Pizza Piccolo (see p. 80/81)

Gas Direct Medium Heat / **Weber® Q™** Direct Medium Heat / **Charcoal** Direct
Prep time 15 minutes / **Grilling time** 7 minutes / **Serves** 8

For the sauce:
3 tablespoons olive oil
3 garlic cloves, coarsely chopped with 1 teaspoon coarse sea salt
2 teaspoons dried Greek oregano
1 teaspoon dried chilli flakes
2 tablespoons sun-dried tomato purée
225g canned diced tomato, drained of juice
¼ teaspoon salt

For the pizza:
8 pitta breads
Olive oil, for brushing
450g fresh mozzarella, cut into 4mm slices
20 snipped fresh basil leaves

1. To prepare the sauce: combine all the ingredients in a food processor or blender and pulse to a coarse sauce consistency. Pour into a medium saucepan, set over a medium heat and bring to a boil, stirring with a wooden spoon. Remove from the heat and let stand while warming the pitta.

2. To prepare the pizza: divide the pitta breads between two foil packages and grill over Direct Medium heat for 4 minutes to warm through. Remove from the packages, brush the bottom surface with olive oil and spoon equal portions of sauce over the top surface. Layer an equal number of mozzarella slices on top and garnish with a sprinkling of basil leaves.

3. Grill over Direct Medium heat for 3 minutes, or until the grilling marks are visible.

4. To serve, give each person a whole pitta or cut the pittas into slices.

Spanish Sizzler

3 small scoops of lemon sorbet
Spanish Cava

Put the sorbet scoops into a chilled goblet. Top up with Cava. Serve with a dessertspoon.

Chorizo in Red Wine

Gas Direct Medium Heat / **Weber® Q™** Direct Medium Heat / **Charcoal** Direct
Prep time 15 minutes + overnight marinating / **Grilling time** 8 to 10 minutes / **Makes** 16

Sixteen 13cm fresh chorizo sausages (about 1.35kg)
Eight 30cm thin baguettes
275g shaved Manchego or other mature hard Spanish cheese

For the marinade:
350ml Rioja, Zinfandel or dry, fruity red wine
3 tablespoons balsamic vinegar
8 allspice berries
8 black peppercorns

1. To prepare the sausages: on one side, prick a dozen small holes with a pin. On the other side make six very shallow score marks along the length, a little over 1.5cm long and evenly spaced.

2. To make the marinade: combine all the ingredients in a large shallow dish and stir. Roll the chorizo in the marinade to cover the surfaces and cover the dish with clingfilm. Refrigerate overnight.

3. Drain the chorizo and discard the marinade. Grill the sausages over Direct Medium heat until fully cooked, 5 to 6 minutes, turning once halfway through grilling time. Should flare-ups occur due to the fat content, switch to Indirect Medium heat for the remaining cooking time.

4. Meanwhile, slice the baguettes partway through the middle, leaving a hinge for easy filling. Divide them between four foil parcels and grill over Direct Medium heat for 3–6 minutes to warm them.

5. To serve, cut each baguette in half, put a sausage inside and sprinkle shavings of cheese on the top.

TIP

Always use long-handled tools for turning meat on the barbecue. Tongs are especially useful for turning food such as sausages. Be careful not to pierce the meat when you are turning it as you will let out all the wonderful flavours.

Chèvre in Vine-leaf Parcels

Gas Direct High Heat / **Weber® Q™** Direct High Heat / **Charcoal** Direct / **Prep time** 20 minutes + 20 minutes rinsing and soaking leaves / **Grilling time** 4 minutes / **Makes** 8

16 vine leaves packed in brine
Olive oil, for brushing
1 crusty baguette
Several cocktail sticks soaked in cold water for 30 minutes

For the filling:
4 tablespoons pine kernels, lightly toasted
225g chèvre cut into 8 slices
50ml pesto

TIP

Remember to rinse the vine leaves thoroughly to remove the intense trace of salt.

1. Rinse the vine leaves under cold running water, then soak in cold water for 15 minutes. Rinse under running water again and repeat, then pat dry with kitchen paper.

2. To make the filling: over a medium heat in a dry non-stick pan toast the pine kernels for 5 minutes, or until they go slightly golden brown and the aroma is released. Remove from the heat and empty into a small bowl.

3. On a clean surface, lay the vine leaves out flat and put a slice of chèvre in the centre. Spread a small dollop of pesto on the cheese and sprinkle over a few pine kernels.

4. Fold the edges of the leaf over the contents and place another leaf on top. Flip the parcel over and fold the ends into the centre in the same fashion. Secure the outer flaps with a presoaked cocktail stick through the corners.

5. Brush the wraps with oil and grill over Direct High heat for 4 minutes, or until the cheese starts to melt. Turn the parcels once halfway through grilling.

6. Meanwhile, wrap the baguette in foil, or brush with oil. Place directly on the cooking grate and warm over Direct High heat for 3 minutes, turning once every minute.

7. To serve, open the parcels, discard the leaves and spread the melted cheese on to crusty baguette. Season.

Grilled Pepper Bruschettas

Gas Direct High Heat / **Weber® Q™** Direct High Heat / **Charcoal** Direct
Prep time 20 minutes + 25 minutes resting / **Grilling time** 27 to 29 minutes / **Makes** 16

For the peppers:
2 large red peppers
2 large yellow peppers
4 tablespoons extra-virgin olive oil, plus extra for basting
1 tablespoon balsamic vinegar
½ teaspoon coarse sea salt
3 tablespoons fresh basil leaves, snipped into strips
225g of shaved pecorino or Parmesan cheese

For the bruschetta:
16 slices of crusty rustic Italian bread 1.5cm thick
3 tablespoons olive oil
2 garlic cloves
½ teaspoon coarse sea salt

1. To prepare the peppers: brush them with oil and grill the whole peppers over Direct High heat until fully charred on the outside – about 25 minutes – turning approximately every 4 to 5 minutes. Transfer to a shallow dish and cover with clingfilm. Leave to cool for an additional 25 minutes.

2. Uncover the dish and scrape off the skin with a paring knife (don't worry if some of it remains). Continue to remove the inner ribs, seeds and stem. Slice the peppers into long strips 2.5cm wide and lay them out on a platter.

3. Drizzle the oil and balsamic vinegar over the top of the peppers, then sprinkle salt and basil over the top. Finish by scattering the cheese on top.

4. To make the bruschetta: brush the bread slices with oil and grill over Direct High heat until browned – about 2 to 4 minutes – turning once halfway through. Place the slices on their sides on a platter, cover loosely with a cloth or towel and leave to cool for 2 minutes. Remove the cloth and rub one side of each with a piece of garlic, drizzle with a little oil and sprinkle with salt.

5. To serve, divide the bruschettas and strips of peppers between eight plates.

Portobello Mushroom Caps

Gas Direct Medium Heat / **Weber® Q™** Direct Medium Heat / **Charcoal** Direct
Prep time 15 minutes / **Grilling time** 8 to 10 minutes / **Makes** 8

**8 large portobello
  mushrooms
8 pieces roasted red pepper
  about 5cm square (see
  page 85)
½ teaspoon chilli powder**

For the filling:
**2 garlic cloves, crushed
  with ½ teaspoon coarse
  sea salt
2 tablespoons extra-virgin
  olive oil
150g ricotta cheese
75g finely grated Parmesan
  cheese
Olive oil, for brushing**

1. To prepare the mushrooms: remove the stalks from the caps and discard. Wipe the surface clean with dampened kitchen paper.

2. To make the filling: put all the ingredients in a non-metallic bowl and stir until well combined.

3. Place a piece of pepper inside each mushroom, then spoon equal portions of the filling so that it is level with the edges of the caps. Season to taste and sprinkle with chilli powder.

4. Brush the underside of each mushroom with oil and grill the mushrooms over Direct Medium heat, rounded-side down, for 8 to 10 minutes, or until browned and tender.

Coq Rouge

**2 parts light rum
1 part gin
1 part freshly squeezed lemon or lime juice
1 part Cointreau or triple sec**

Stir or shake all the ingredients with cracked ice. Strain into a chilled cocktail glass and serve straight up. Garnish with a twist of orange peel.

Pork Souvlaki in Pitta Bread

Gas Direct High Heat / **Weber® Q™** Direct High Heat / **Charcoal** Direct
Prep time 15 minutes + overnight marinating / **Grilling time** 8 minutes / **Makes** 8

900g pork tenderloin
Vegetable oil, for brushing
½ teaspoon coarse sea salt
8 pitta breads
Lemon wedges

For the marinade:
75ml olive oil
115ml dry white wine
4 garlic cloves, crushed
3 bay leaves
1 tablespoon dried oregano,
crumbled

TIP
Remember to oil the
metal skewers before
threading the meat,
as it makes removal
much easier.

1. To make the marinade: combine all the ingredients in a medium bowl and stir well. Leave to rest at room temperature until the pork is ready to marinate.

2. Cut the pork into 2cm cubes. Lay them in a large shallow dish, pour over the marinade and toss the meat until the surfaces are fully coated. Cover with clingfilm and refrigerate overnight.

3. When ready to grill, drain the pork and discard the marinade. Thread the skewers through the centre of each pork cube and brush the surfaces with the oil.

4. Grill the pork over Direct High heat until fully cooked, about 8 minutes, or 3 minutes each side. Sprinkle salt over the top.

5. Meanwhile, snip a thin layer off the top of each pitta bread, making it easy to fill. Divide them between four foil packages, or brush them with oil and place them directly on the cooking grate and grill over Direct High heat for 4 minutes to warm them.

6. To serve, divide the meat from each skewer into a pitta. Squeeze over some lemon juice and season with salt. As an additional treat, prepare some tzatziki, a yogurt dressing containing cucumber, fresh mint, cracked black pepper and a little garlic. Fresh onion and sprigs of dill or coriander also make a delicious garnish.

Entrecôte in Ciabatta

Gas Direct High Heat / **Weber® Q™** Direct High Heat / **Charcoal** Direct
Prep time 15 minutes / **Grilling time** 8 minutes / **Makes** 8

**4 rib-eye or sirloin steaks,
trimmed of fat, about 225g
each and 2cm thick
8 small ciabattas or crusty
white rolls**

For the seasoning:
**3 tablespoons herbes de
Provence (or an Italian
herb mix if not available)
1 teaspoon freshly cracked
black pepper
¼ teaspoon salt**

For the butter baste:
**115g butter
3 garlic cloves, crushed
1 tablespoon Worcestershire
sauce
1 tablespoon lemon juice**

1. To prepare the seasoning: grind the herbs, pepper and salt in a pestle and mortar or crush by hand until fine in texture and aromatic.

2. Rub the steaks with the seasoning, then leave to rest at room temperature while preparing the butter baste.

3. To make the butter baste: melt the butter over a medium heat, then add the garlic and sauté until it becomes translucent – about 2 minutes. Add the other ingredients and cook for a further 2 minutes. Remove from the heat and leave to rest at room temperature while starting the grill.

4. Grill the steaks over Direct High heat until medium rare, roughly 8 minutes, turning once halfway through grilling time and basting with the butter sauce throughout. Transfer the steaks to a chopping board and loosely cover with foil.

5. Meanwhile, slice the ciabattas lengthways, leaving one side hinged so that it opens like a book. Brush the insides with the remaining butter baste and grill the outer crust over Direct High heat for browning – about 1 to 2 minutes.

6. Slice each steak at a 45-degree angle from one end to another and divide between the ciabattas.

Limoncello Italiano

2 parts vodka or citron vodka
½ part lemon juice
½ part sugar syrup
Lemonade

Shake the vodka, lemon juice and sugar syrup in a cocktail shaker with cracked ice. Strain into a highball glass half-filled with crushed ice and a long curled length of lemon peel. Top up with lemonade.

Moulin Rouge

4 parts pineapple juice
½ part brandy
Champagne or sparkling wine

Shake the pineapple juice and brandy thoroughly in a cocktail shaker with cracked ice. Strain into a highball glass, half-filled with crushed ice. Top up with champagne or sparkling wine and stir.

Bellini

3 parts chilled dry champagne
1 part chilled peach juice
1 peach slice, to garnish

Pour the champagne and peach juice into a chilled champagne saucer glass. Stir lightly with a glass swizzle stick. Garnish with a thin slice of peach.

Sol y Sombre

1 part anisette
1 part brandy

Pour the anisette into a shot glass and carefully add the brandy, over the back of a bar spoon so that it sits on top of the anisette.

CHAPTER FIVE

Around The Globe

Smoky Baba Ghanoush

Gas Direct Medium Heat / **Weber® Q™** Direct Medium Heat / **Charcoal** Direct
Prep time 15 minutes + 20 minutes cooling / **Grilling time** 32 to 42 minutes / **Serves** 8

16 pitta breads
1 lemon wedge
1 tablespoon extra-virgin olive oil, for drizzling
½ teaspoon hot paprika

For the dip:
2 large aubergines
4 garlic cloves, coarsely chopped with 1 teaspoon coarse sea salt
3 tablespoons tahini
3 tablespoons extra-virgin olive oil
3 tablespoons fresh lemon juice
½ teaspoon coarse sea salt
Salt and freshly ground black pepper

1. To prepare the dip: grill the aubergines over Direct Medium heat for 30 to 40 minutes, or until they have deflated. Turn them periodically to char the whole of the surface. Be careful not to puncture the aubergines while turning them.

2. Remove the aubergines from the grill and leave to cool for 20 minutes on a chopping board.

3. While the aubergines are cooling, grill the pitta breads on both sides for a total of 2 minutes to crisp and brown them slightly. Remove them from the grill and slice into quarters. Place the aubergines in a napkin-lined basket to stay warm.

4. Slice open the aubergines and scoop out the softened flesh into a food processor or blender, discarding the charred skin. Add the remaining dip ingredients and process to a smooth consistency. Adjust the taste with additional salt.

5. To serve, spoon the dip into an earthenware bowl. Squeeze the lemon wedge over the top, drizzle with the oil and sprinkle with paprika. Offer round the baba ghanoush with the basket of pitta bread.

Seared Squash Salad

Gas Direct High Heat / **Weber® Q™** Direct High Heat / **Charcoal** Direct
Prep time 15 minutes / **Grilling time** 8 minutes / **Serves** 8

2 medium yellow zucchini
   squash
2 patty pan squash
Olive oil, for brushing
¼ teaspoon coarse sea salt
Freshly cracked black
   pepper
175g Greek feta cheese

For the dressing:
8 tablespoons extra-virgin
   olive oil
1 teaspoon Dijon mustard
2 tablespoons lemon juice
4 garlic cloves, crushed
2 teaspoons dried oregano
Salt and freshly ground
   black pepper

1. To prepare the dressing: whisk the oil, mustard and lemon juice together in a small bowl. Add the garlic and oregano and stir until evenly distributed. Leave at room temperature while the squash is grilled.

2. Slice the squash lengthways into strips about 6mm thick. Brush them with oil, season to taste and grill over Direct High heat until brown marks appear on both sides – about 8 minutes. Remove and lay flat on a large serving platter.

3. To serve, crumble the feta cheese over the squash and then drizzle with the dressing. Pass the platter round along with crusty white loaf to soak up the dressing.

Red Sky at Night

Dash of freshly squeezed
   lemon juice
Lemonade
½ part crème de cassis

Fill a chilled highball glass with ice and add a good dash of lemon juice. Pour in the lemonade almost to fill the glass and stir in the crème de cassis.

Tamarind Glazed Salmon

Gas Direct Medium Heat / **Weber® Q™** Direct Medium Heat / **Charcoal** Direct
Prep time 20 minutes / **Grilling time** 8 to 10 minutes / **Makes** 8

**8 pieces of salmon fillets
with skin on, 75g each
and 2.5cm thick
1 tablespoon ground cumin
8 iceberg lettuce leaves**

For the glaze:
**6 tablespoons tamarind
paste
1 whole ripe banana, cut
into pieces
1 tablespoon soy sauce
1 tablespoon olive oil
1 small red chilli, deseeded
¼ teaspoon salt**

TIP

If you experience a
flare-up whilst grilling,
don't attempt to
extinguish it with water.
Closing the lid will
reduce the oxygen
and eliminate the
flare-up.

1. To prepare the salmon: run your fingers over the flesh surface of the fish to check for bones and remove any with tweezers. Rinse the salmon fillets under cold running water and pat dry with kitchen paper.

2. Place in a shallow dish and rub the cumin all over the salmon. Allow to rest at room temperature for 20 minutes while you make the glaze.

3. To make the glaze: place all the ingredients in a food processor or blender and process until completely smooth. Pour the sauce into a medium saucepan, bring to the boil over a high heat and then reduce to a simmer. Cook for 5 minutes, then remove from the heat.

4. Brush each piece of fish with the glaze, then grill, skin-side down, over Direct Medium heat until cooked through, 8 to 10 minutes, turning once after 3 to 4 minutes, or when the skin is crispy.

5. To serve, brush with remaining glaze and roll up in lettuce leaves.

Prosciutto & Pineapple Wraps

Gas Direct Medium Heat / **Weber® Q™** Direct Medium Heat / **Charcoal** Direct
Prep time 15 minutes / **Grilling time** 12 to 14 minutes / **Makes** 32

1 large ripe pineapple
32 slices of prosciutto
Fresh basil leave, to garnish
(optional)

For the butter sauce:
50g butter, melted
2 tablespoons lime juice
1 tablespoon soft brown
sugar
1 teaspoon cayenne pepper

1. To prepare the pineapple: remove the bottom and the spiky top. Standing it upright on a chopping board and remove the outer skin and eyes in downward strokes of a sharp knife. Slice the pineapple into eight rings of equal thickness. Remove the dense centre of each ring with a paring knife.

2. In a shallow bowl, combine the sauce ingredients and stir well. Dip each ring in the sauce and set on Direct Medium heat until sizzling brown – about 6 to 7 minutes per side. Brush with the remaining sauce and turn over with tongs, as necessary.

3. To make the wraps: remove from the grill and transfer to a chopping board. Slice each ring into quarters. Wrap a piece of prosciutto around each quarter and skewer with a cocktail stick.

4. To serve, arrange on a platter, garnished with fresh basil leaves, if desired.

2 parts tequila
5 parts orange juice
½ part grenadine

Tequila Sunrise

Pour the tequila and orange juice into a highball glass filled with ice. Stir. When it settles, pour the grenadine in a circle around the top of the drink and let it fall to the bottom. Garnish with a slice of orange and a maraschino cherry.

Chicken Tikka on Naan Pillows

Gas Direct Medium Heat / **Weber® Q™** Direct Medium Heat / **Charcoal** Direct
Prep time 20 minutes + 1 hour marinating / **Grilling time** 8 minutes / **Makes** 32

**675g skinless chicken
breast or thigh fillets**
Eight 20cm naan breads
**3 tablespoons melted
butter, for basting**
**8 tablespoons home-made
sweet chutney, to serve**

For the marinade:
4 garlic cloves, crushed
**4 tablespoons of Indian
tikka spice mix (or curry
powder)**
3 tablespoons lemon juice
225g natural yogurt

TIP
Always ensure that your barbecue is sited on level ground – never use a grill that wobbles or seems unstable.

1. To prepare the marinade: combine all the ingredients and stir until well mixed. Set aside at room temperature while preparing the chicken.

2. Rinse the chicken thoroughly under cold running water and pat dry with kitchen paper. Cut into strips 2.5 x 10cm long and place in a shallow dish. Pour the marinade over the chicken and toss until fully coated. Cover with clingfilm and refrigerate for 1 hour.

3. Remove the chicken from the refrigerator and discard the marinade.

4. Before grilling the chicken, separate the naan breads and divide them between two foil packages or brush them with oil and place directly on the grill. Grill over Direct Medium heat for 4 minutes to warm them.

5. Grill the chicken over Direct Medium heat until fully cooked – about 4 minutes. Brush the surfaces with butter and turn once halfway through the grilling time.

6. To serve, slice each naan into quarters and place in a cloth-lined basket to keep warm. Fill a small bowl with chutney and place in the centre of a platter. Arrange the chicken around the bowl. Guests can then make their own 'naan pillows', setting a piece of chicken on top of a piece of naan and garnishing it with a dab of chutney.

Tandoori Lamb Skewers

Gas Indirect Medium Heat / **Weber® Q™** Direct Low Heat / **Charcoal** Indirect
Prep time 15 minutes + overnight marinating / **Grilling time** 6 to 8 minutes / **Serves** 8

**900g boneless lamb
shoulder, fat trimmed**
**2 tablespoons melted
butter**
Eight 10cm naan breads
Coarse sea salt
**8 tablespoons home-made
sweet chutney, to serve**

For the marinade:
1 litre natural yogurt
3 tablespoons lemon juice
**3 garlic cloves, coarsely
chopped**
**4 tablespoons garam
masala or Indian spice
paste**

1. To make the marinade, blend all the ingredients until well mixed and creamy.

2. Cut the lamb into 2.5cm cubes. Lay them in a large shallow dish, pour over the marinade and toss the meat until the surfaces are fully coated. Cover with clingfilm and refrigerate overnight.

3. When ready to grill, drain the lamb and discard the marinade. Thread the lamb on to 8 metal skewers. Melt the butter and reserve for basting.

4. Before grilling the lamb, separate the naan breads and divide them between two foil packages and grill over Indirect Medium heat (or Direct Low heat on the Weber® Q™) for 4 minutes to warm through.

5. Grill the lamb over Indirect Medium heat (or Direct Low heat on the Weber® Q™) until fully cooked, 6 to 8 minutes for medium rare to medium, turning once halfway through. Brush surfaces with melted butter 2 to 3 times while cooking.

6. Remove from the grill, transfer to a serving platter and sprinkle salt over the top. Slice each naan in half and keep warm. Arrange the lamb around a bowl of chutney and serve it with the naan bread for guests to make their own wraps.

Spiced Minced-beef Kebabs

Gas Direct High Heat / **Weber® Q™** Direct High Heat / **Charcoal** Direct
Prep time 25 minutes + 1 hour chilling / **Grilling time** 10 to 12 minutes / **Makes** 8

450g each freshly minced chuck and sirloin steak or 900g lean minced beef
Olive oil
Coarse sea salt
8 pitta breads
Several wooden skewers soaked in cold water for 30 minutes

For the seasoning:
1 onion, finely chopped
Small handful of fresh mint leaves, finely chopped
2 teaspoons ground cumin
2 teaspoons ground coriander
1 teaspoon freshly cracked black pepper
½ teaspoon cayenne pepper

1. To prepare the seasoning: combine all the ingredients in a bowl and mix well.

2. Add the beef, kneading and squeezing until the seasoning is thoroughly mixed in with the meat. Divide the mixture into eight equal portions. With wet hands, roll each portion into a ball.

3. Brush the skewers with oil and thread them through the centre of each ball. Roll the balls into a sausage shape around each skewer, moulding them so they are about 12.5cm long and 2.5cm in diameter. Cover with clingfilm and refrigerate for 1 hour.

4. Before grilling the kebabs, place a folded piece of foil directly on the grill and under the exposed wood of the skewers to help prevent burning. Brush the kebabs with oil and grill over Direct High heat until fully cooked – about 6 to 8 minutes – turning once halfway through grilling time.

5. Meanwhile, snip a thin layer off the top of each pitta. Divide them between four foil packages and grill over Direct High heat for 4 minutes to warm them.

6. To serve, put two kebabs in each pitta bread. You could also top with thinly sliced onion, tomato and finely shredded lettuce. Or prepare a yogurt and cucumber-based dressing, like tzatziki, if desired.

Rusty Nail

2 parts Scotch whisky
1 part Drambuie
1 long lemon twist, to garnish

Combine ingredients with ice in a mixing glass and stir. Strain into an old-fashioned glass filled with ice. Garnish with a long twist of lemon peel.

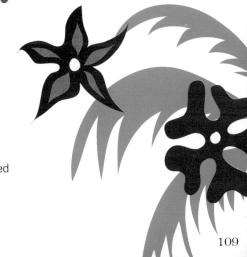

Rising Sun

2 parts vodka
2 parts freshly squeezed
  grapefruit juice
½ part passion fruit syrup
½ lemon, juice only
½ pink grapefruit slice, to garnish

Shake all of the ingredients together in a cocktail shaker and strain over ice on a large old-fashioned glass. Garnish with a slice of pink grapefruit.

Mint Haze
(non-alcoholic)

2 teaspoons sugar
5 fresh mint leaves
1 dash of freshly squeezed lime juice
Sparkling apple juice

Crush the sugar and mint leaves in a pestle and mortar. Frost the rim of an old-fashioned glass by dipping it in water then in the mint sugar. Put a little more mint sugar in the glass, with 3 to 4 ice cubes. Add a dash of lime juice, then top up with sparkling apple juice.

Almond Breeze

1 part white rum
1 dash of Amaretto or orgeat syrup
½ part melon liqueur
Tonic water

Shake the rum and liqueurs in a cocktail shaker with cracked ice. Strain into a highball glass, half-filled with crushed ice. Top up with tonic water.

Acapulco Gold

2 parts pineapple juice
1 part grapefruit juice
1 part tequila
1 part golden run
1 part coconut milk

Combine all the ingredients in a cocktail shaker with cracked ice. Shake well. Strain into a Boston glass half-filled with ice cubes. Garnish with a fun straw and a monkey in a palm tree.

Kiwi Kraze

3 parts kiwi fruit juice
1 part gin
1 dash of absinthe
Tonic water
Kiwi slices, to garnish

Shake the kiwi juice, gin and a good dash of absinthe in a cocktail shaker with cracked ice. Strain into an old-fashioned glass half-filled with crushed ice. Top up with tonic water. Garnish with a slice of kiwi fruit.

Index